This Book Belongs to ....

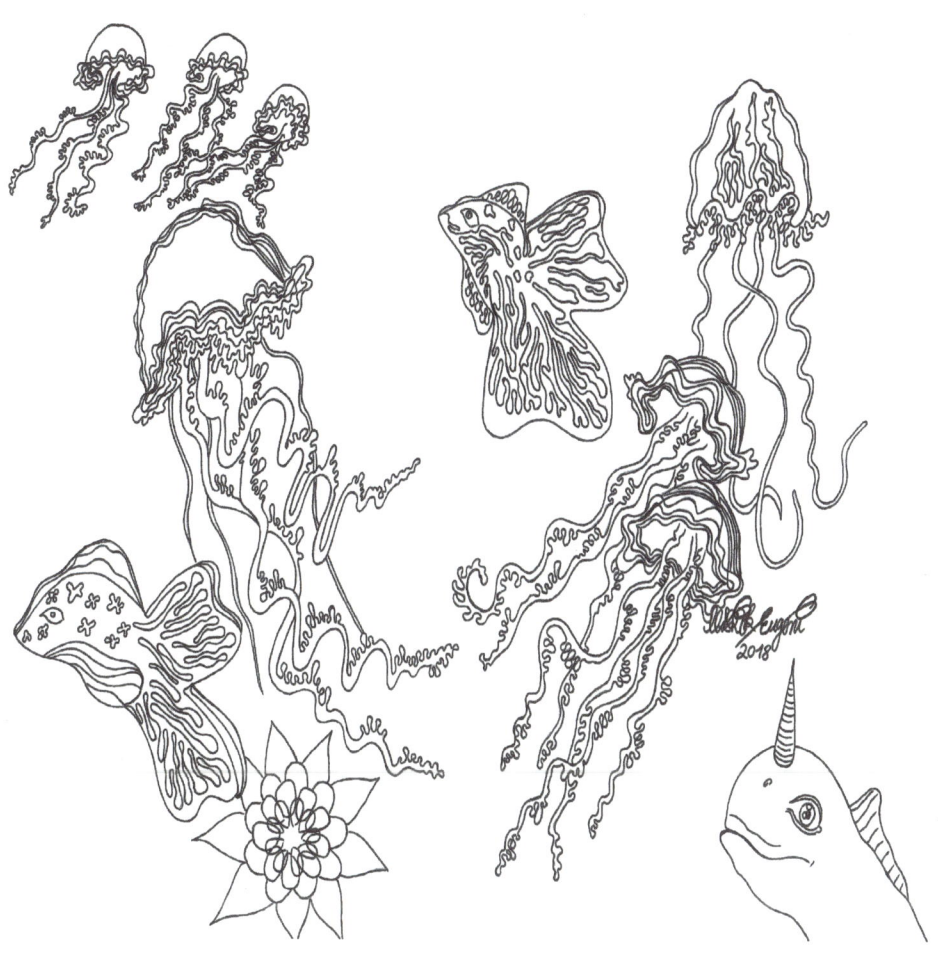

Anything & Outer Limits

Marjgeni

Marja Eugeni Abbas

Welcome

To

Art

Anything & Outer Limits   Marjgeni   VOL1

Warning :

It is stricktly prohibited to recreate any of this Images
 in any form for sale !!!!!!!!
All Images and Texts from Bookcover through all
the interior pages are
under Copyright © by Marja Eugeni Abbas in 2018.
All rights reserved.

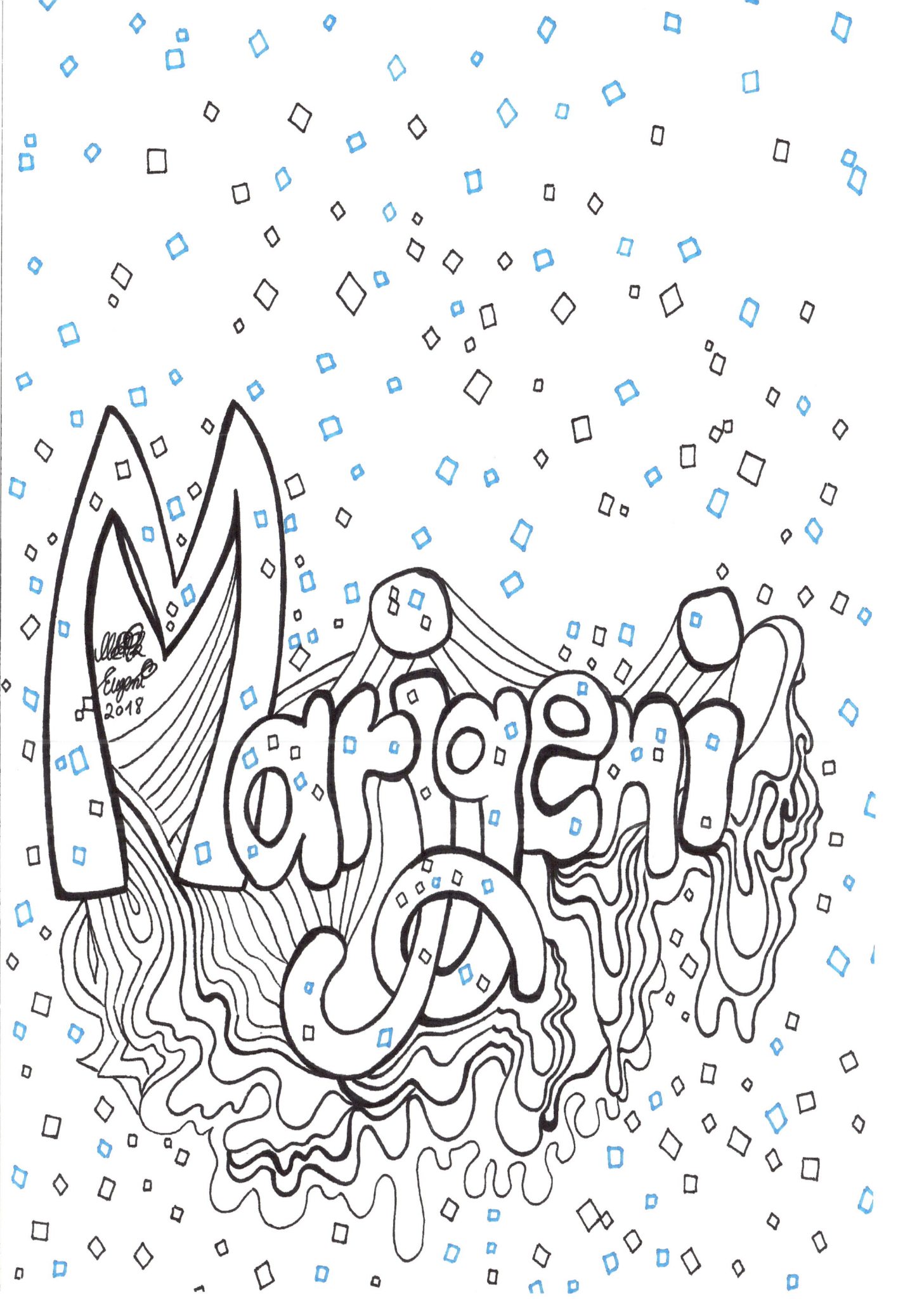

Art is a different Dimension it carries your Heart

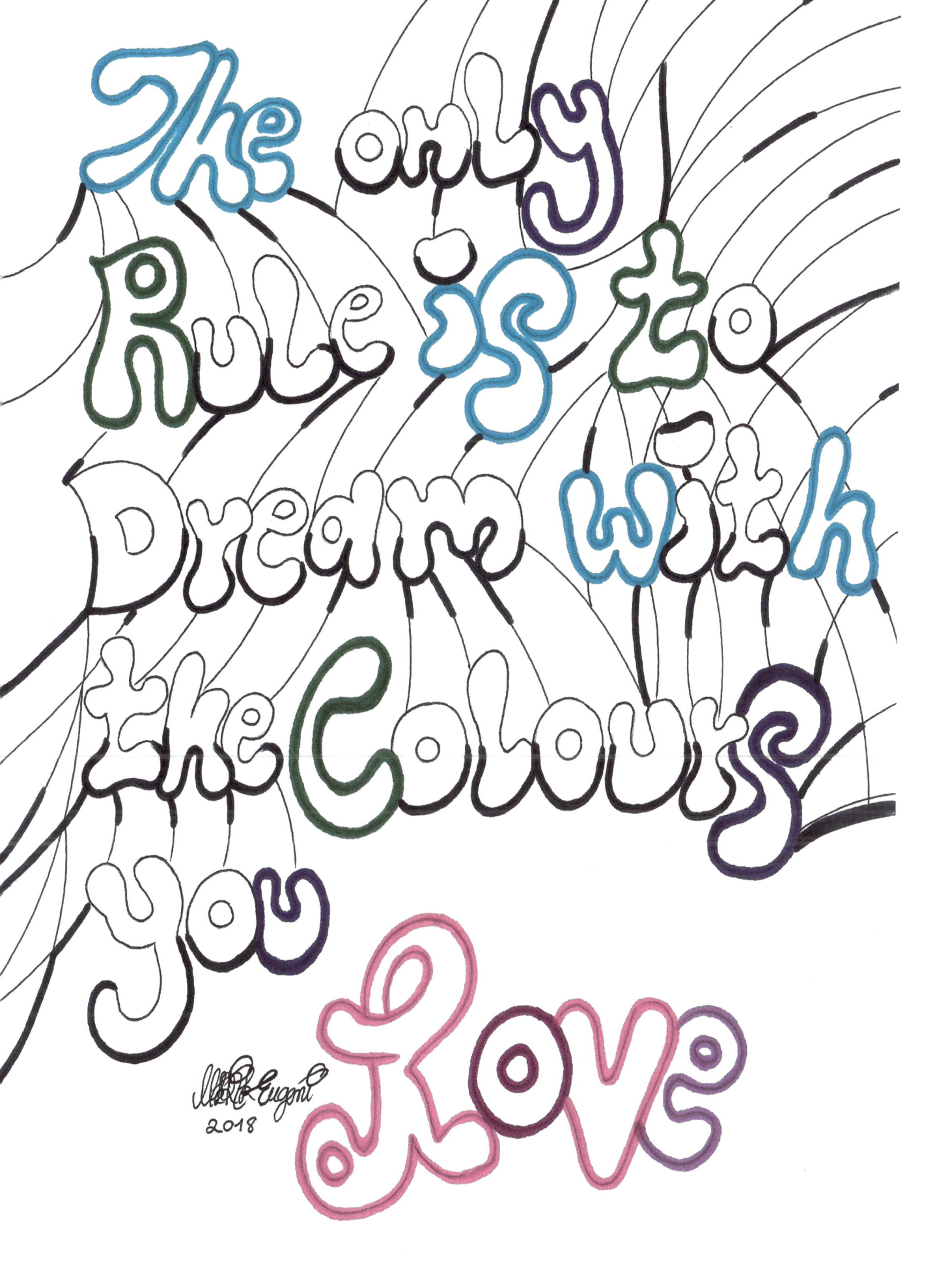

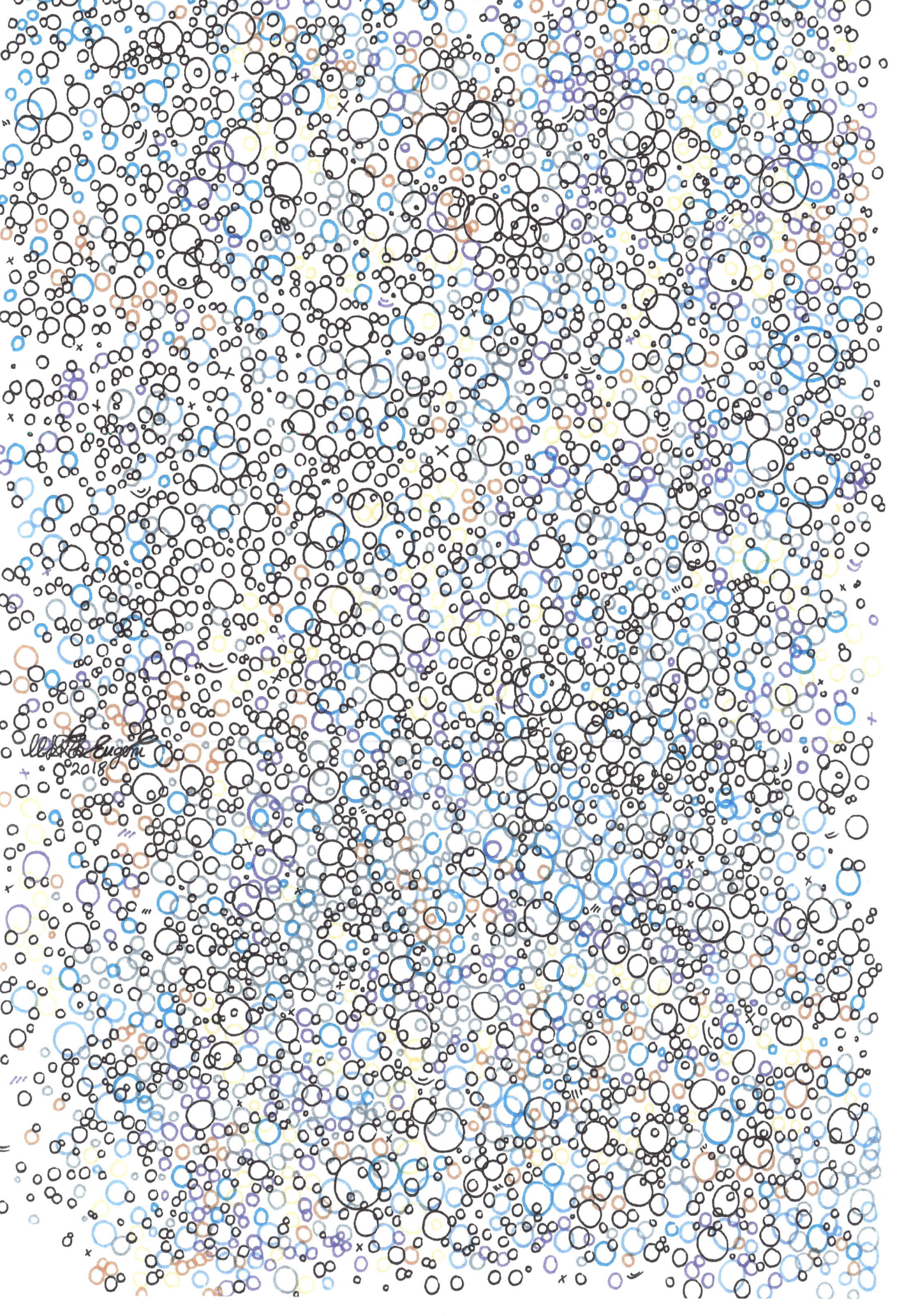

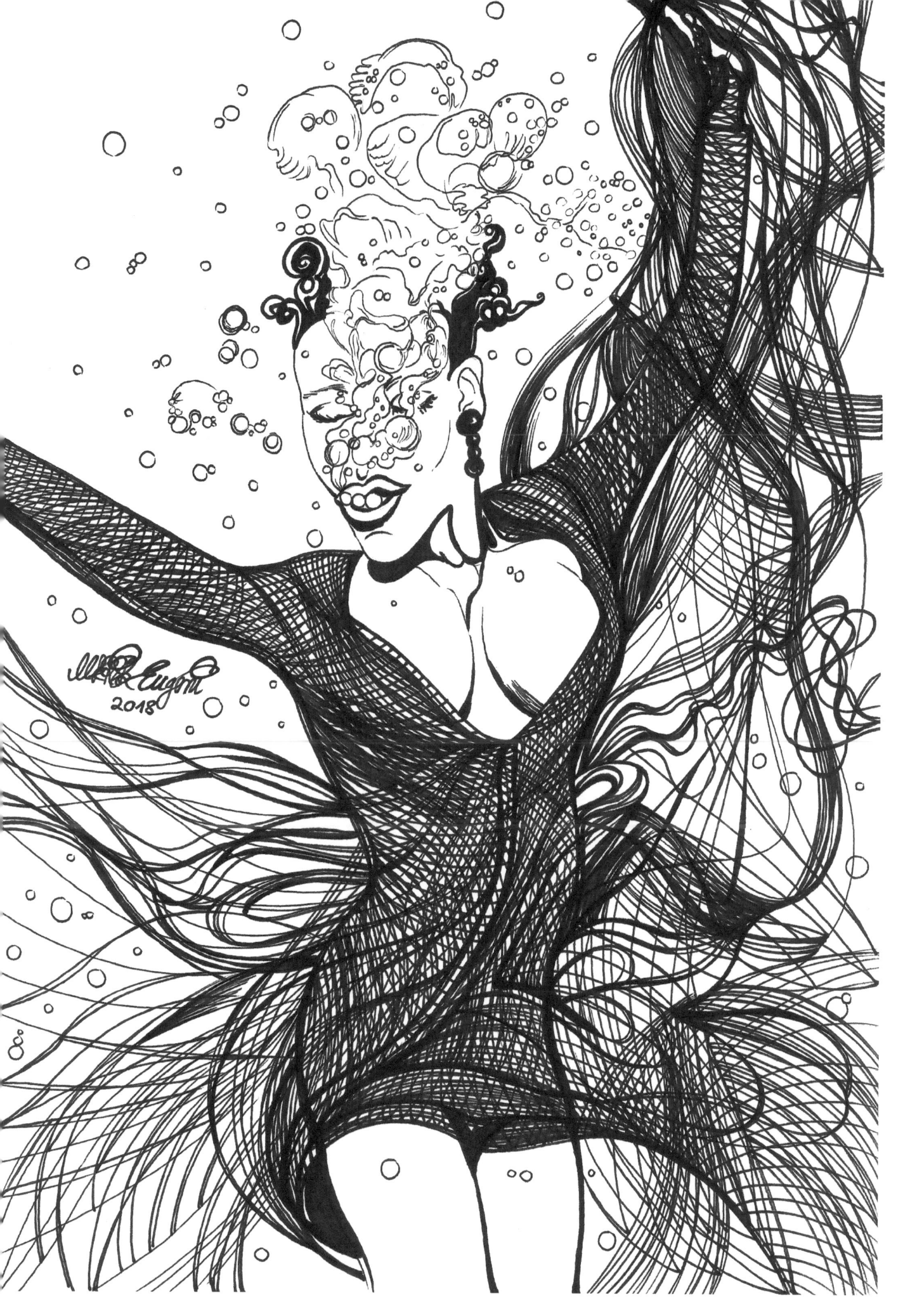

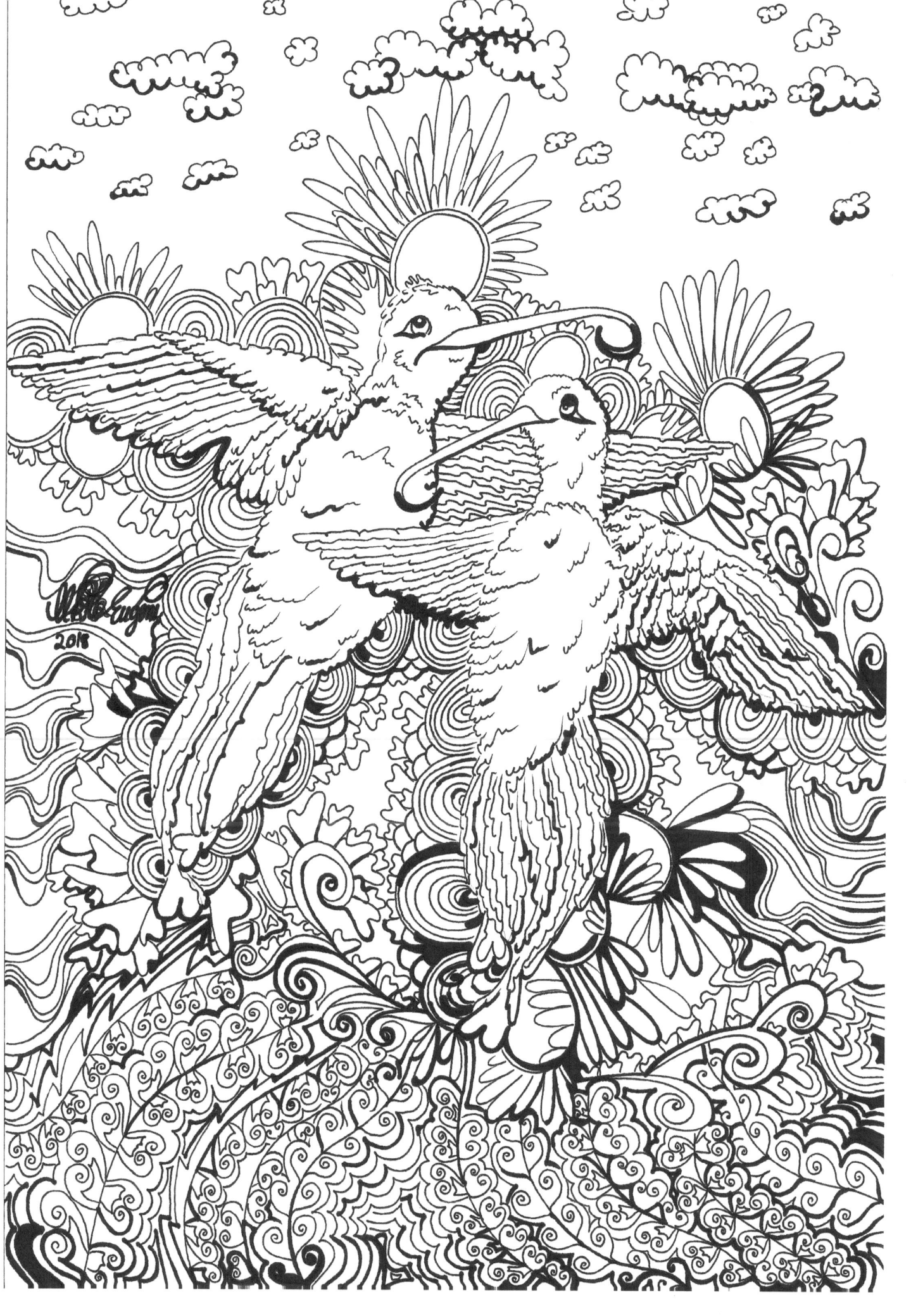

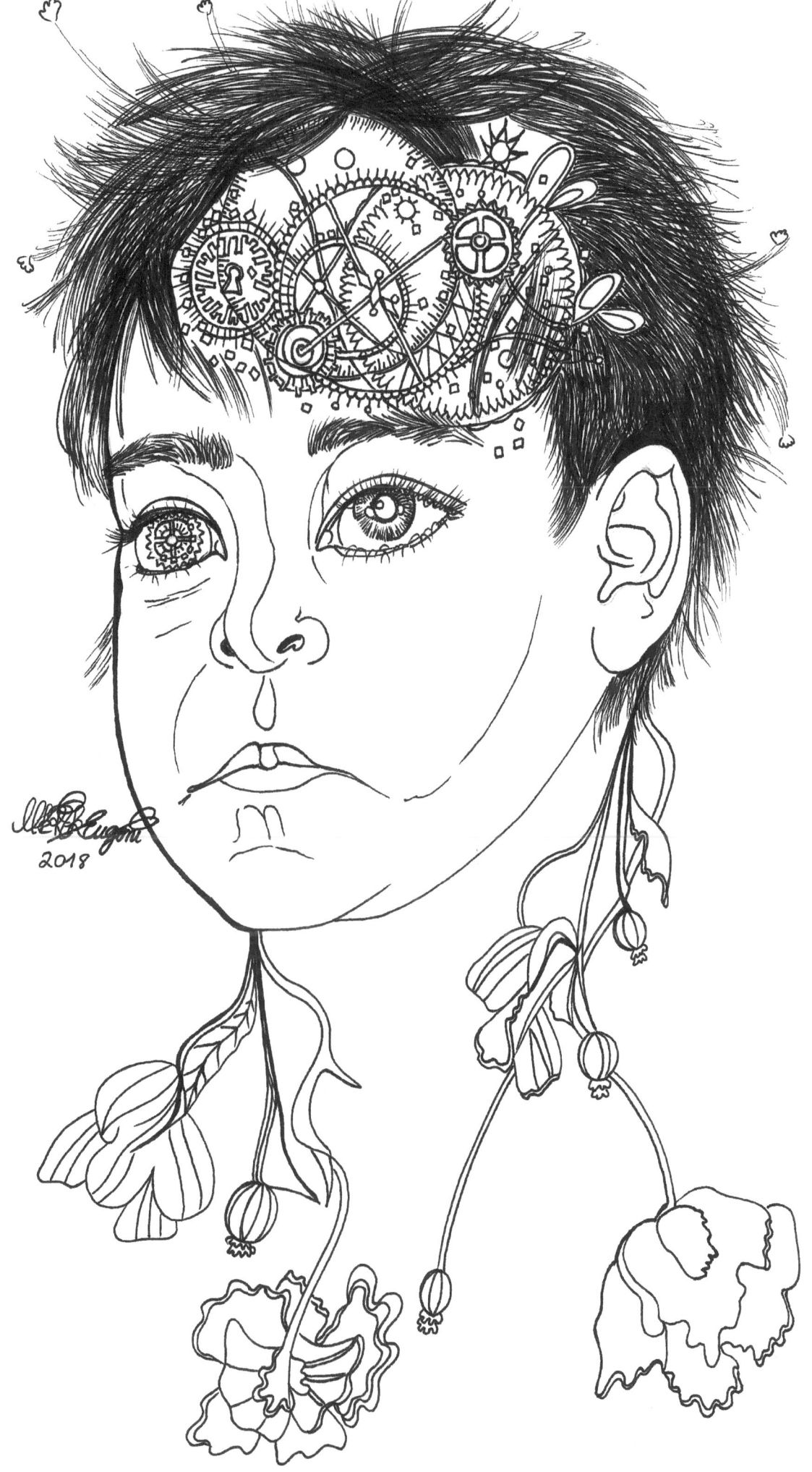

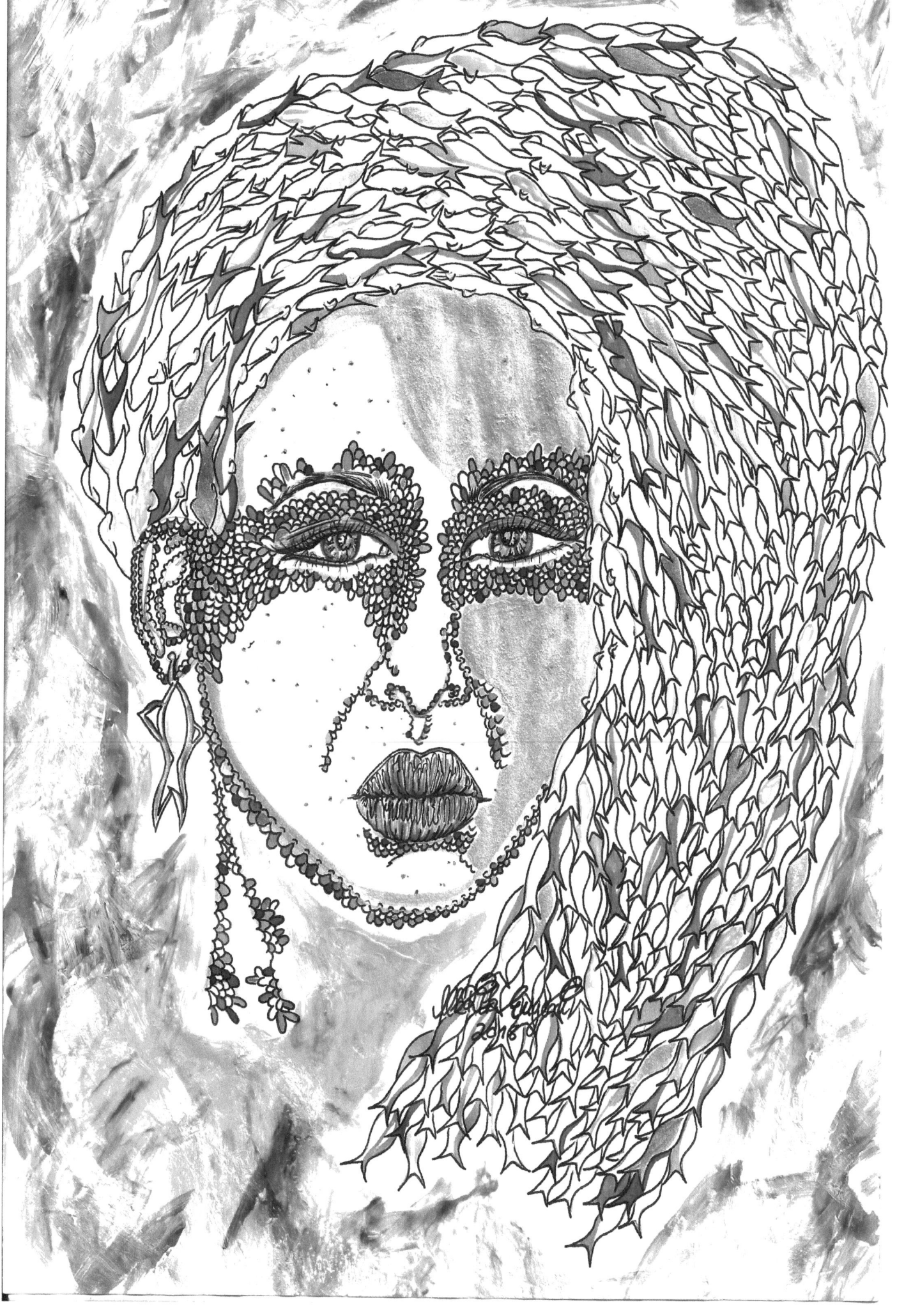

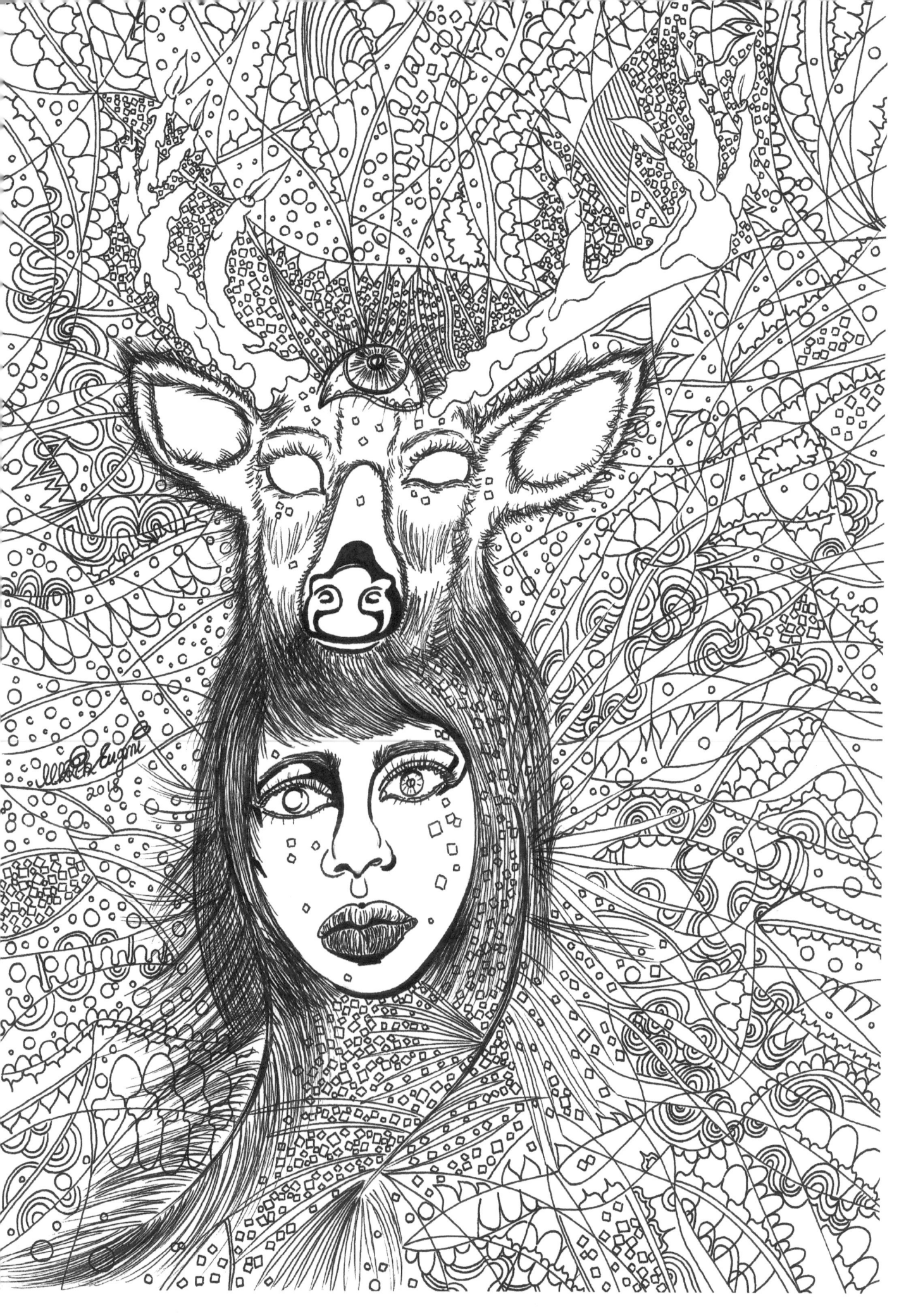

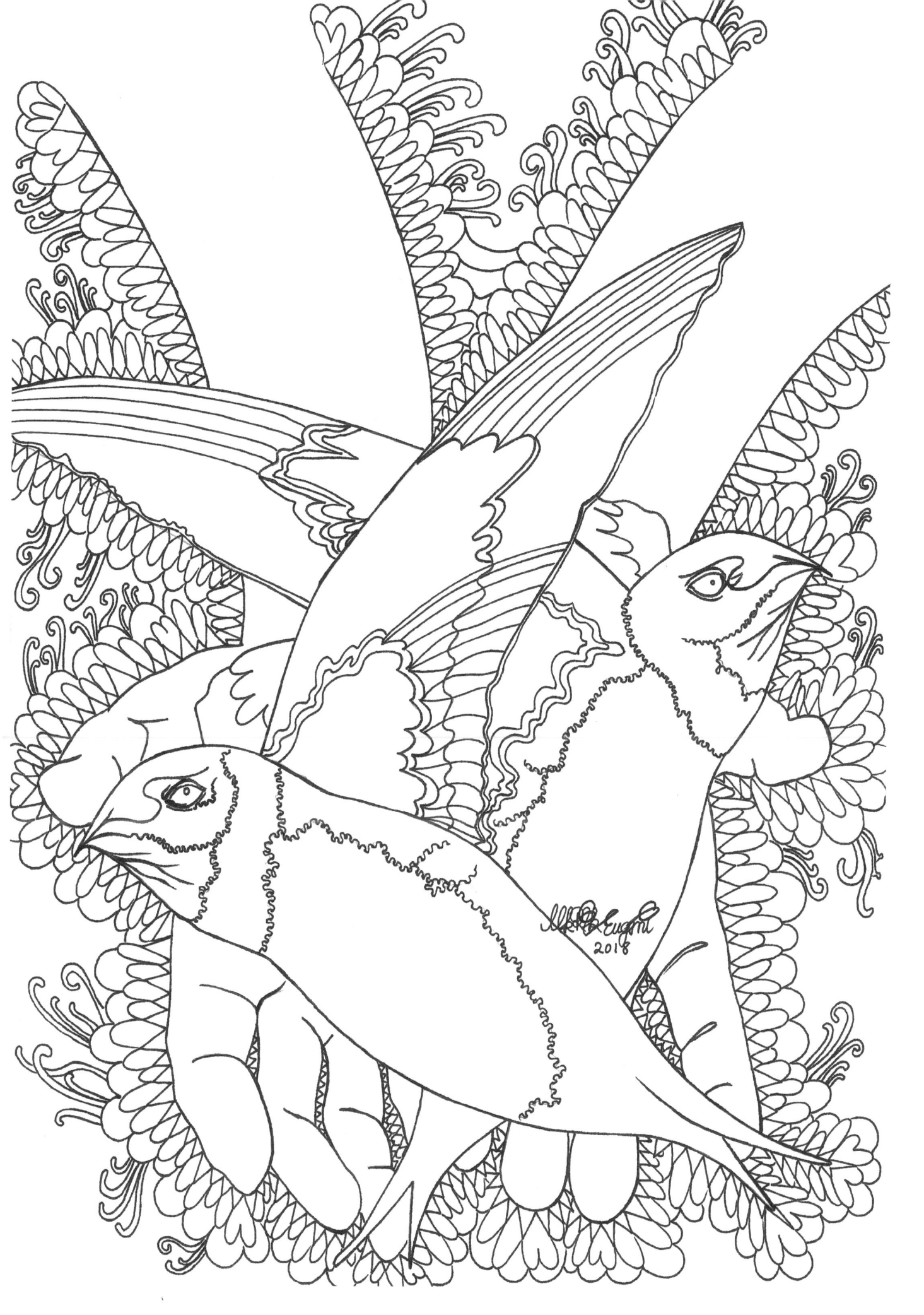

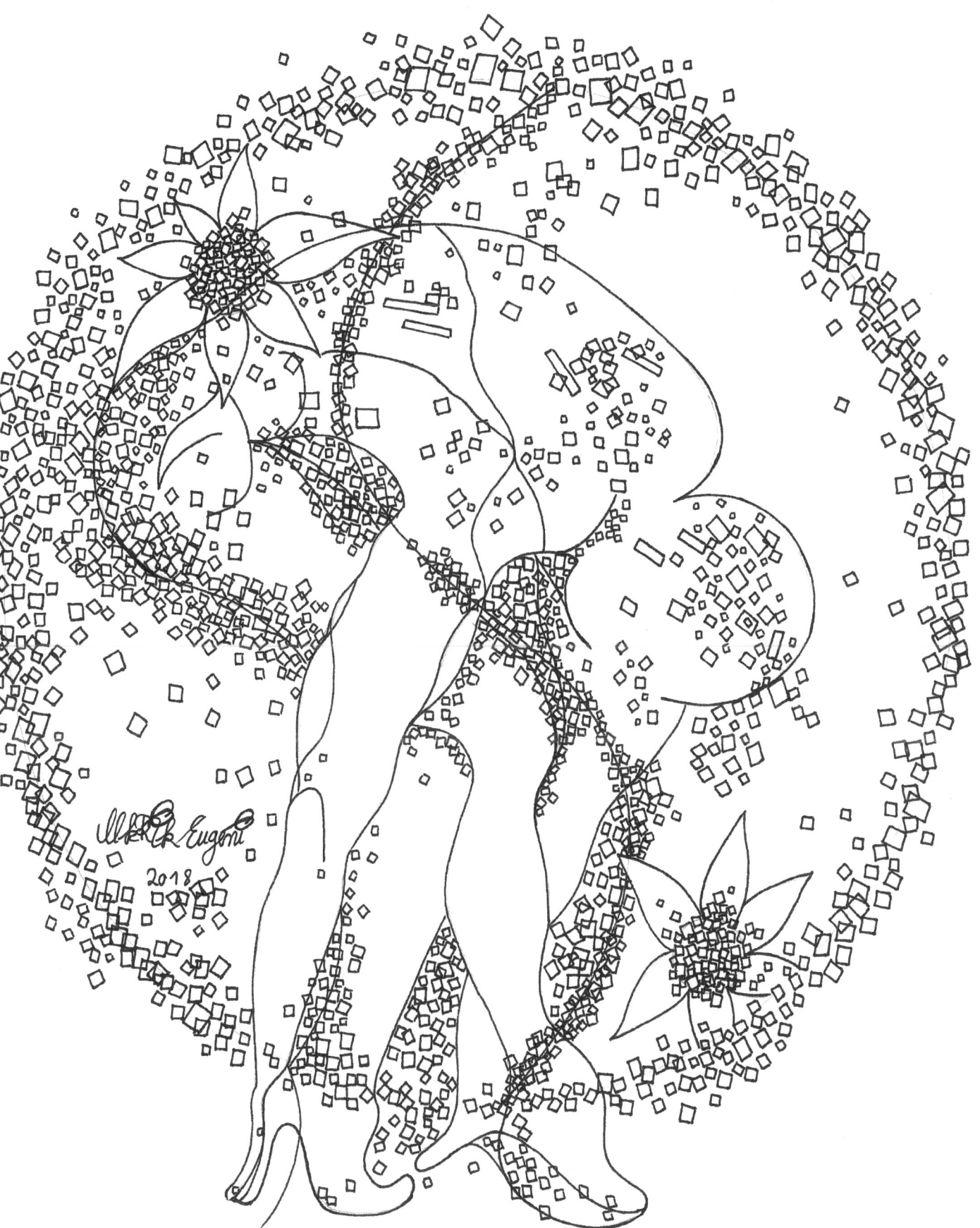

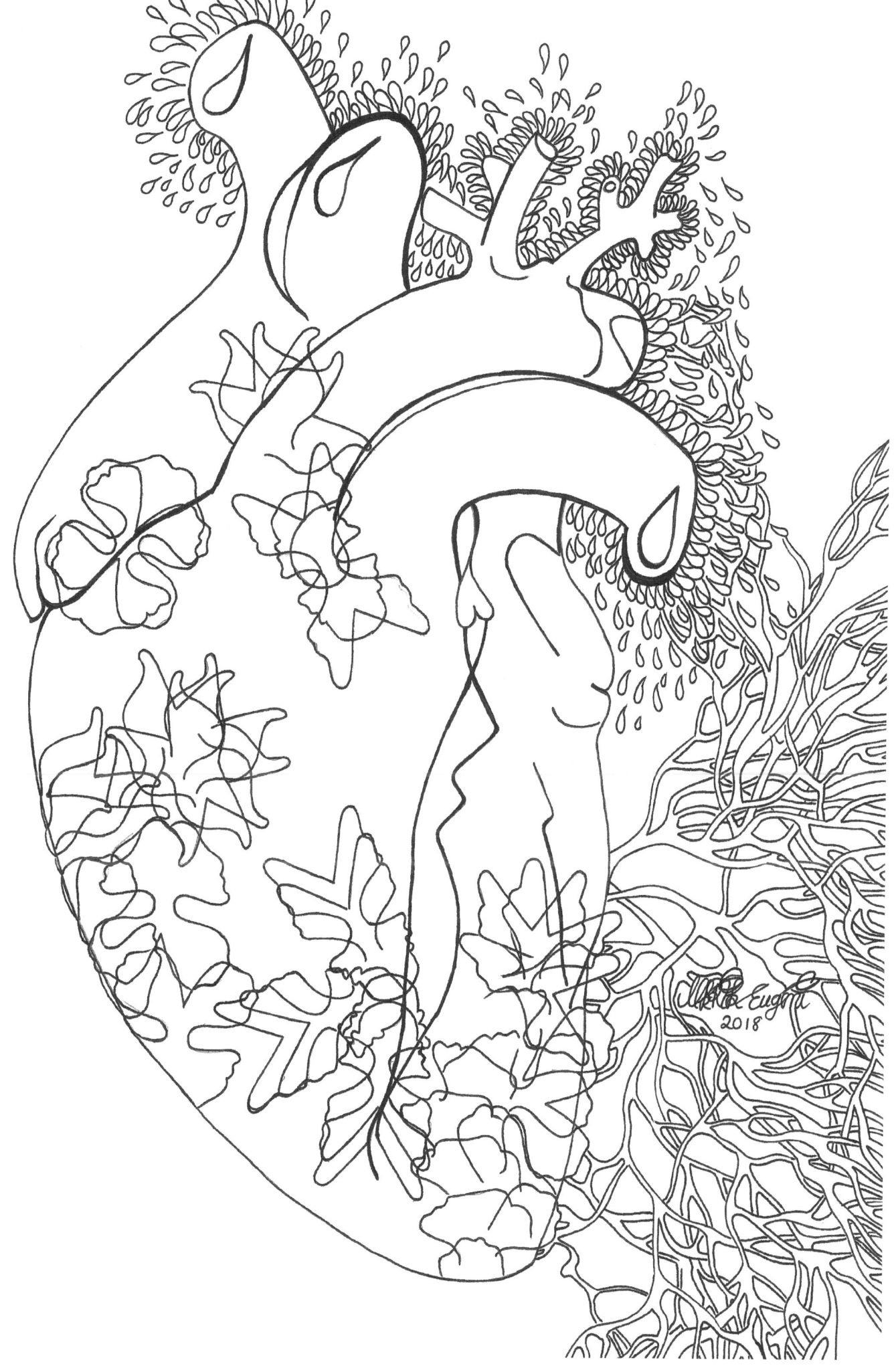

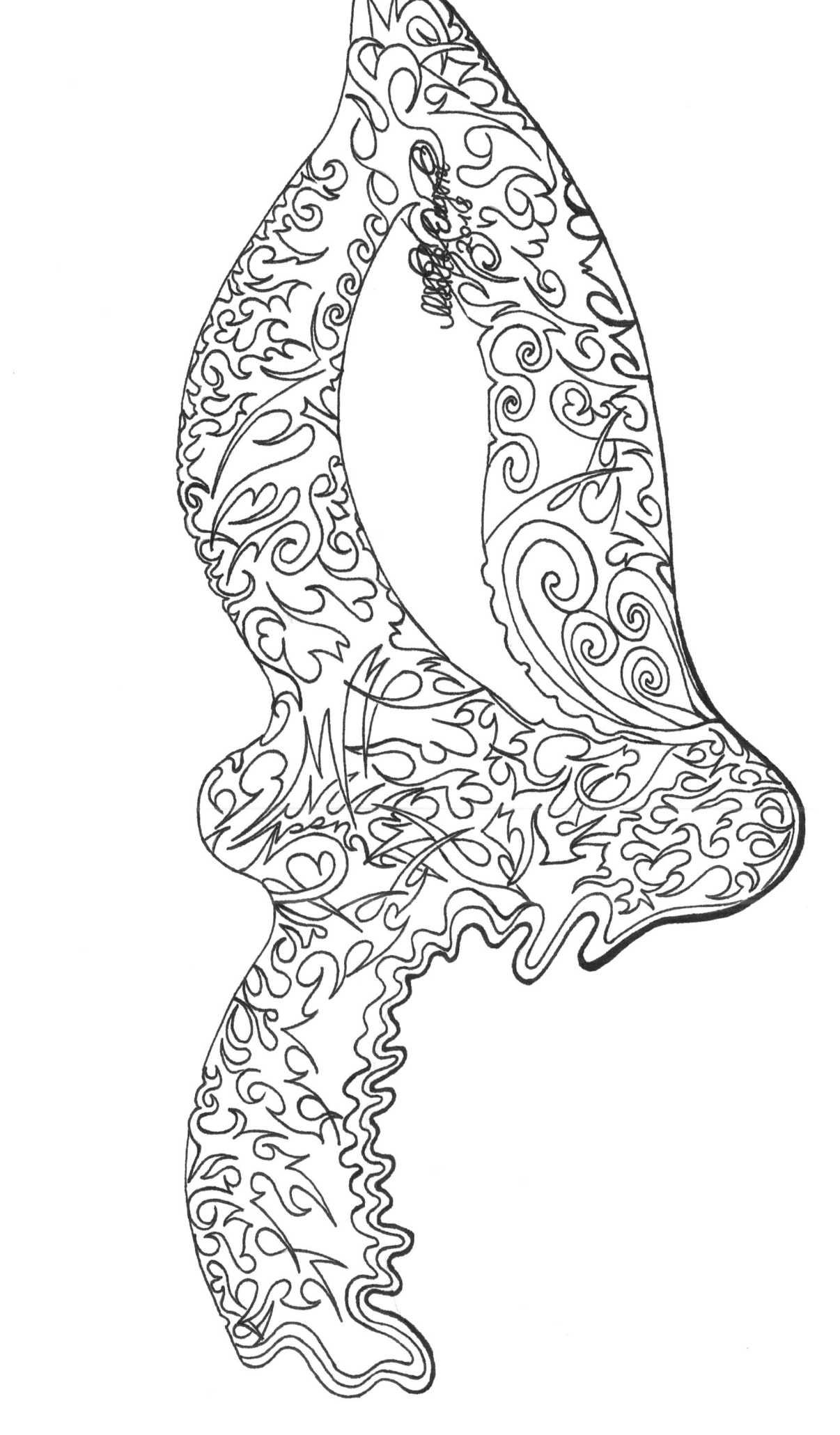

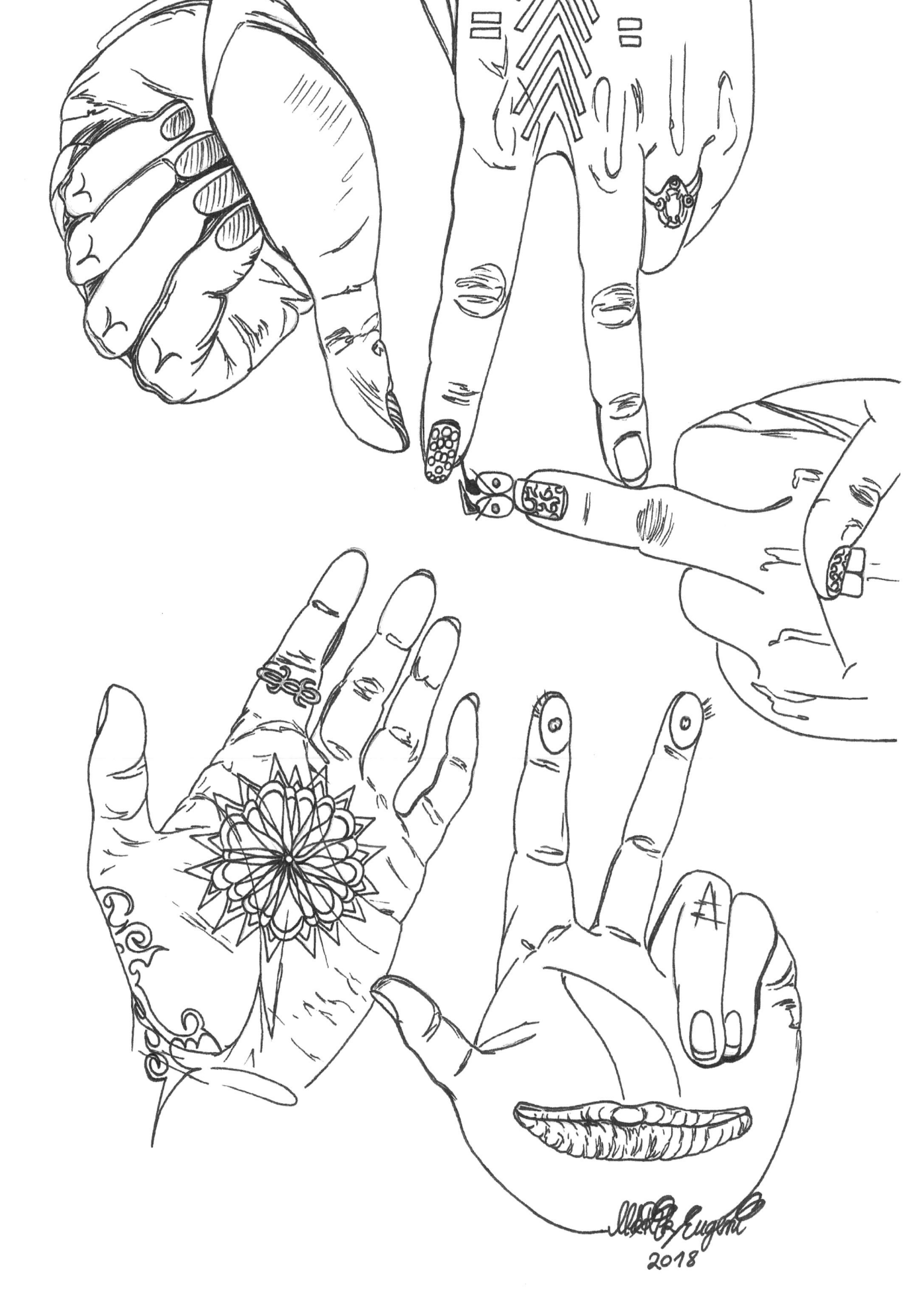

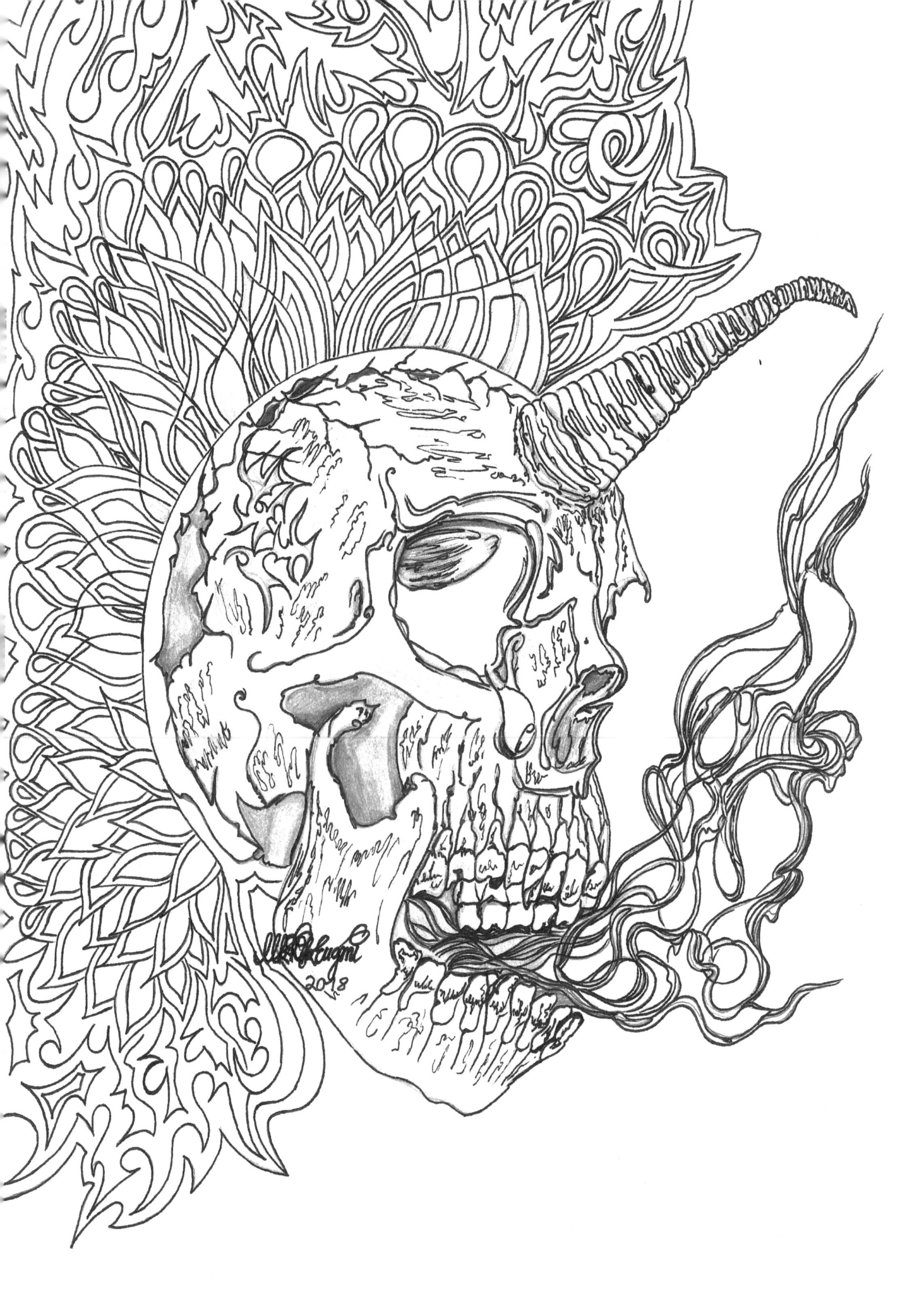

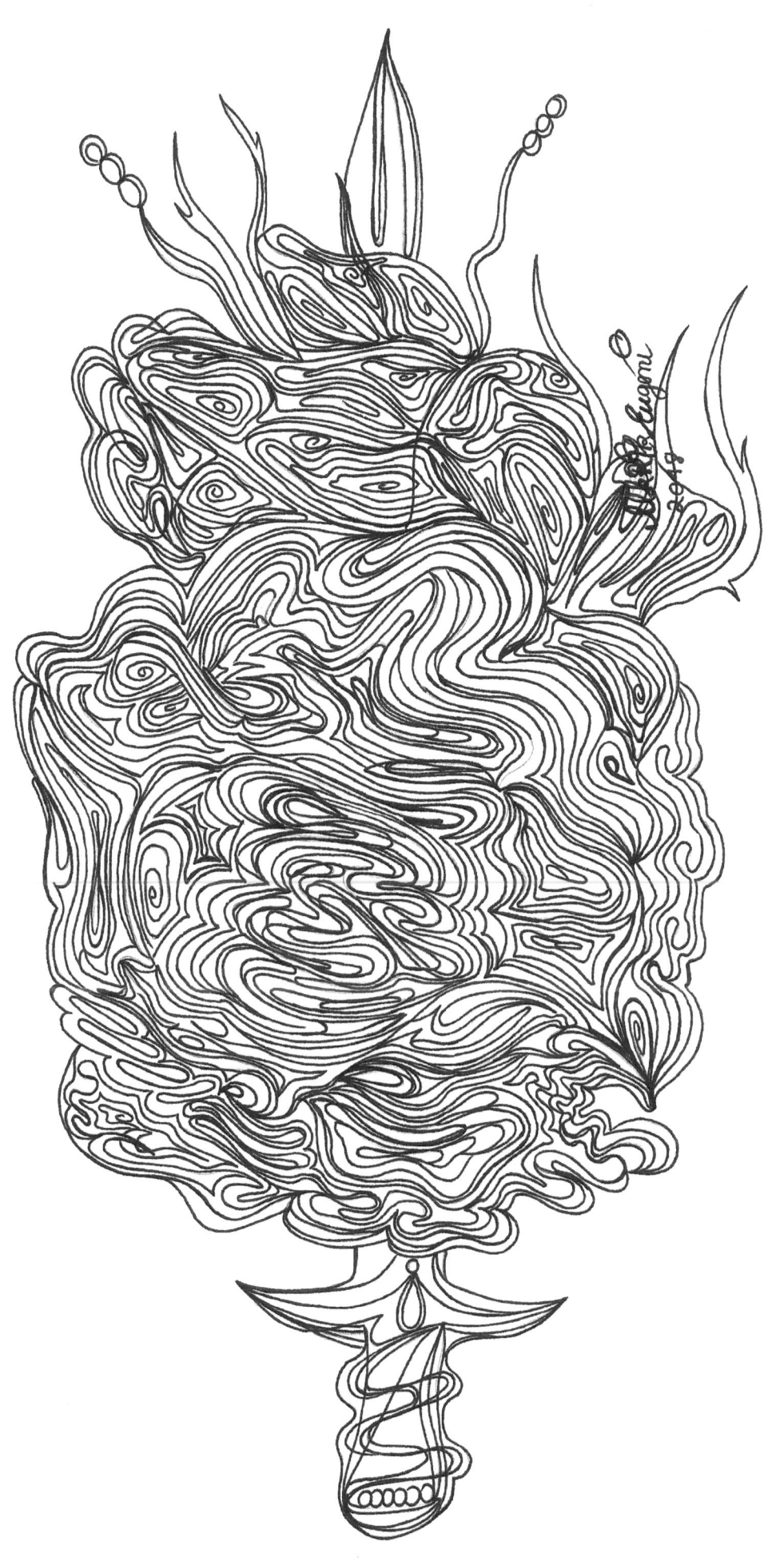

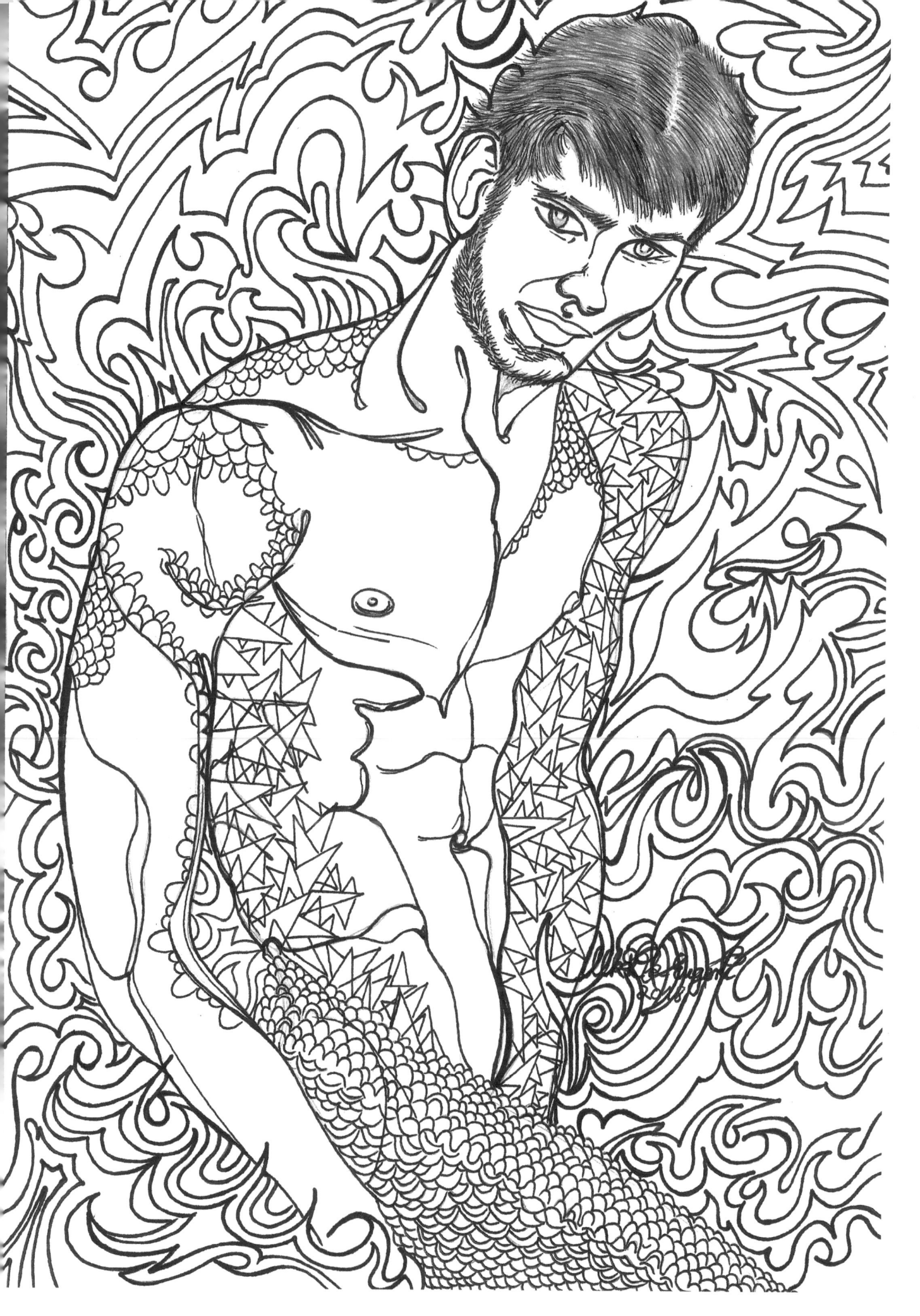

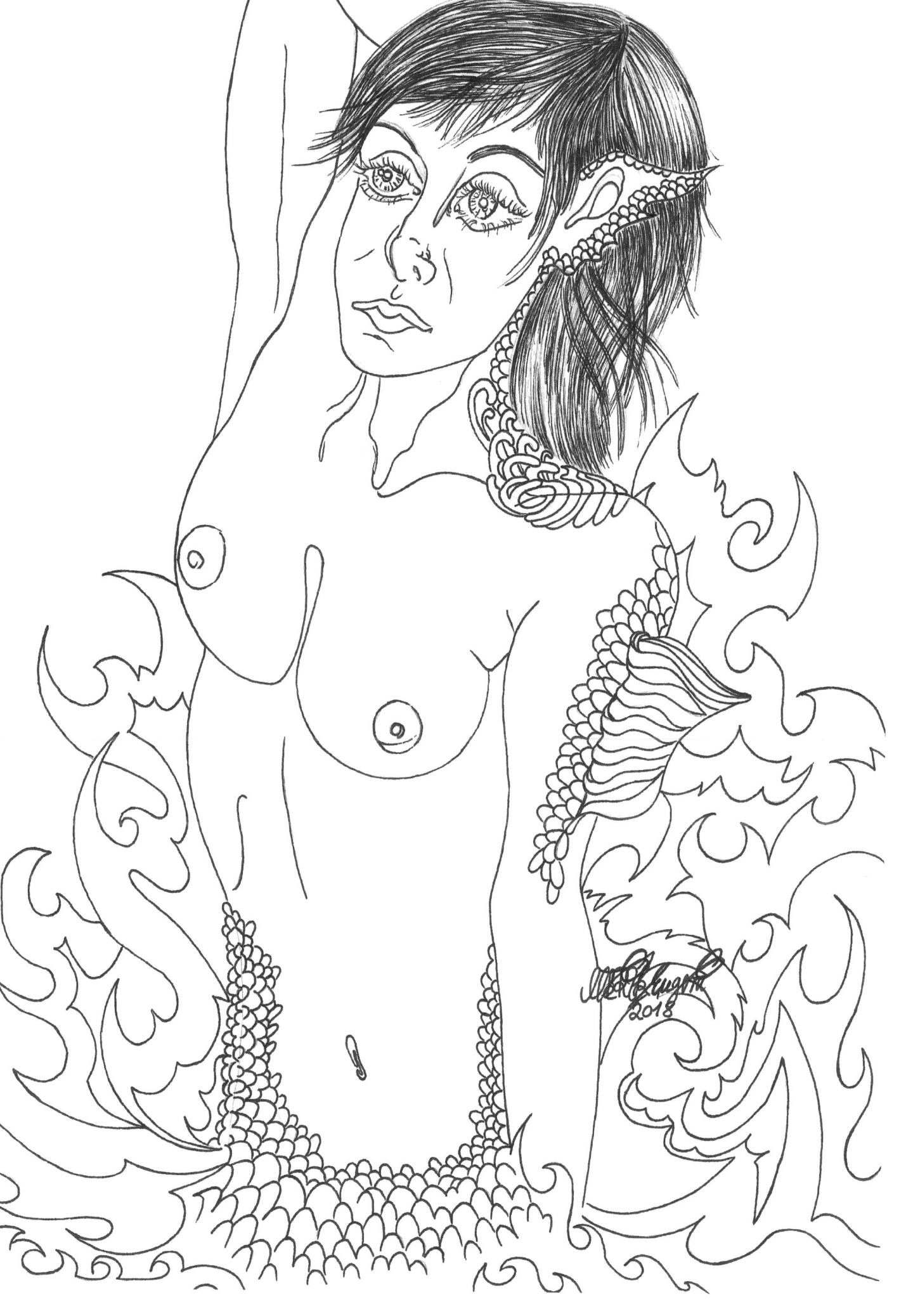

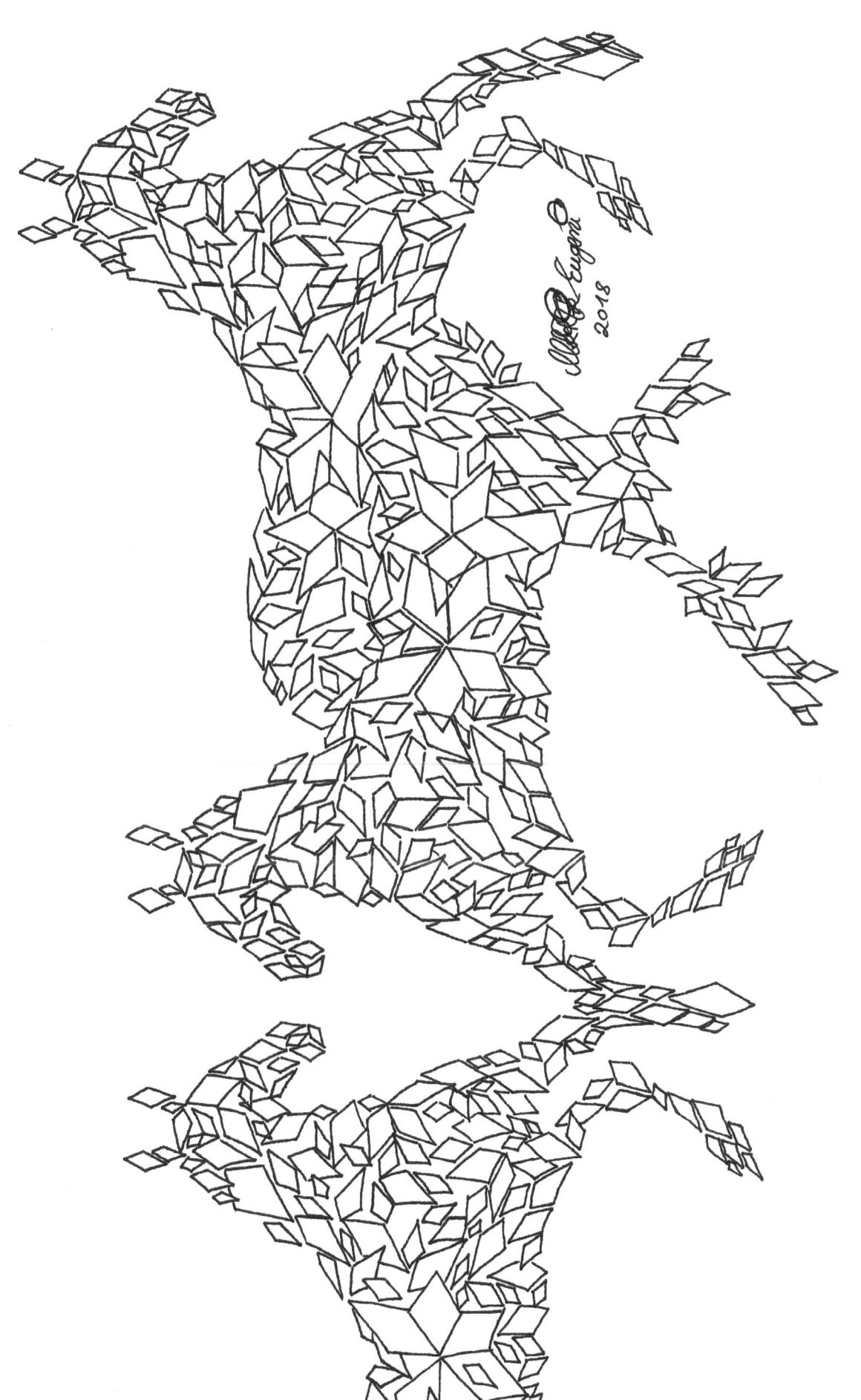

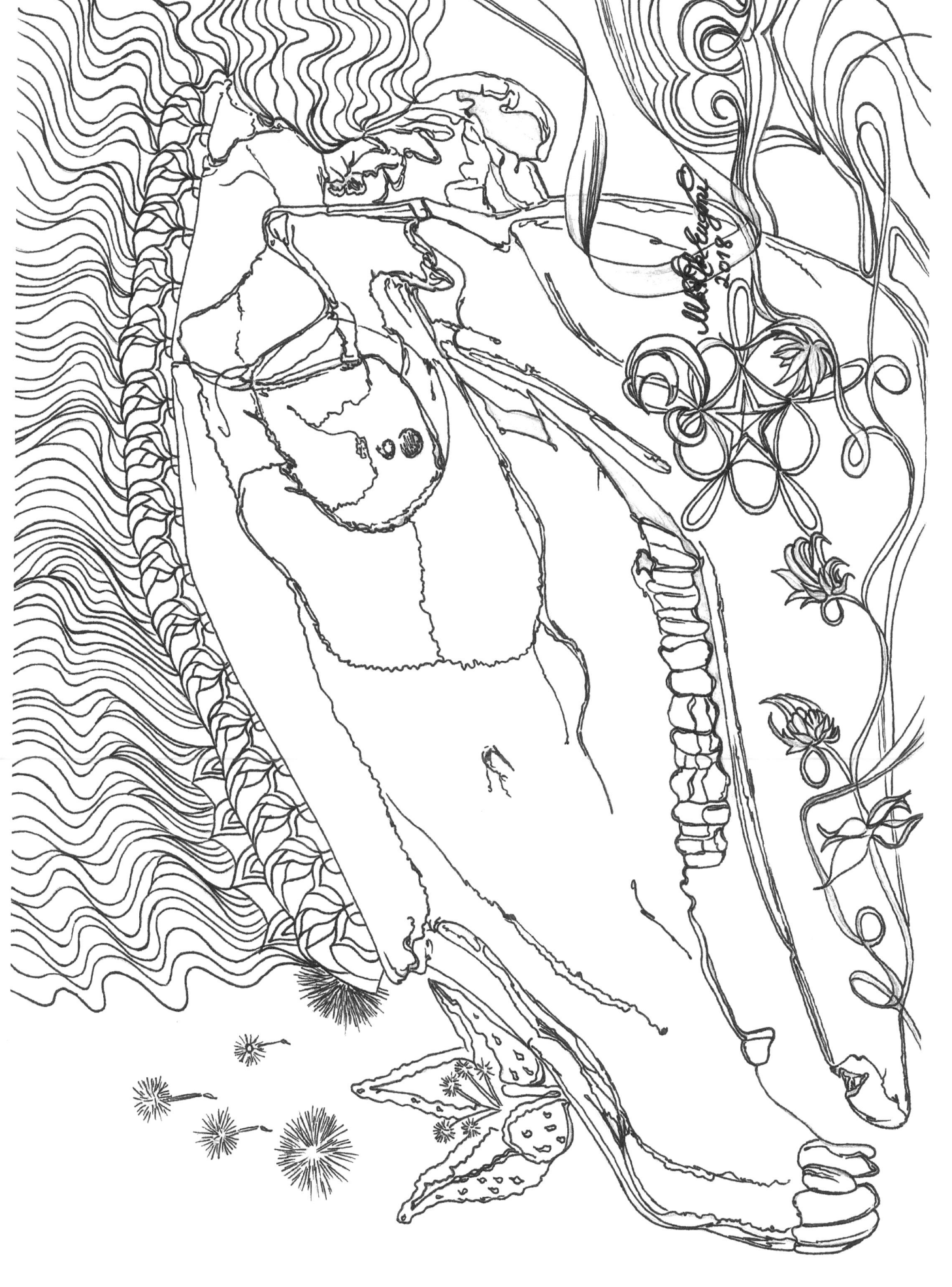

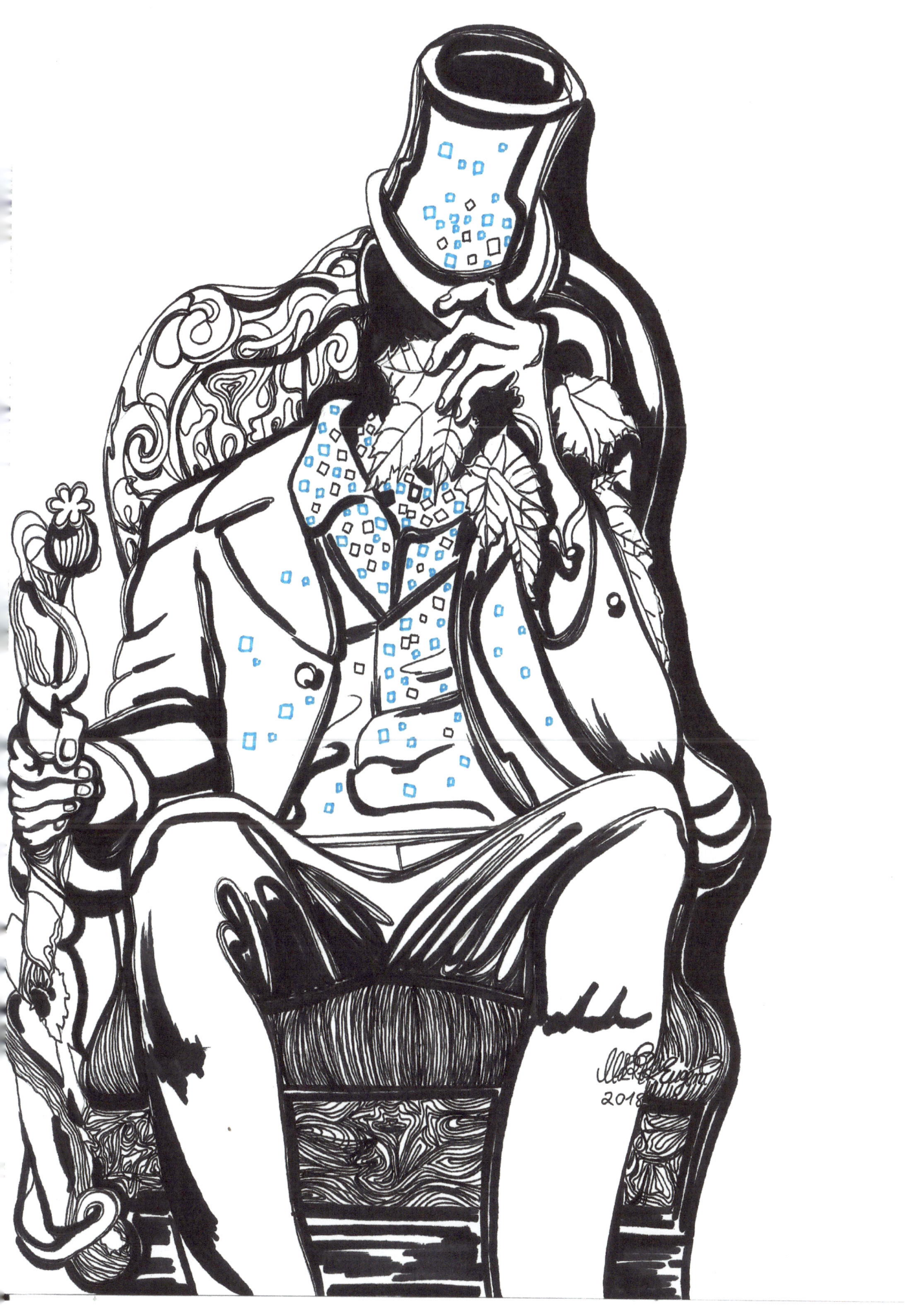

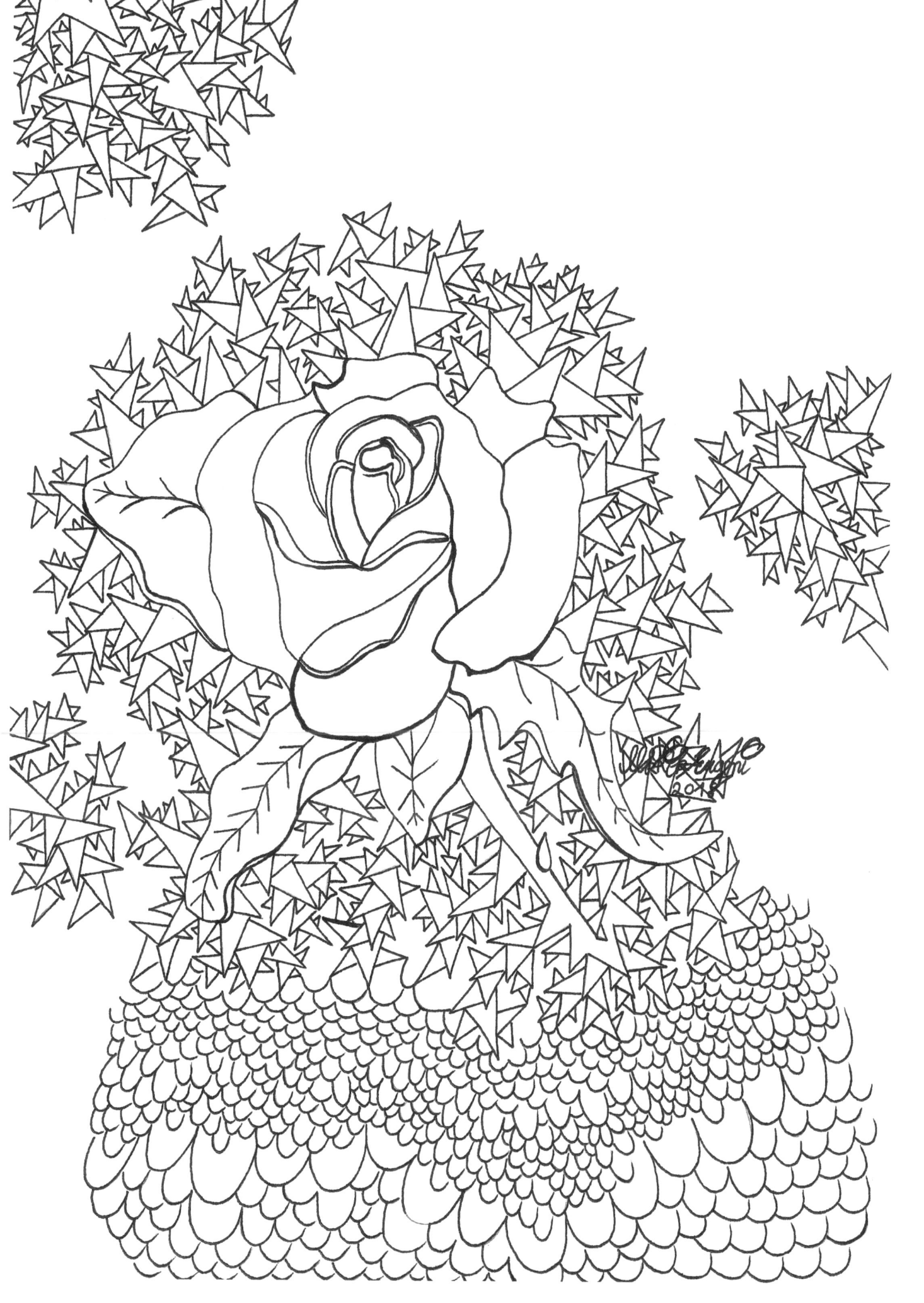

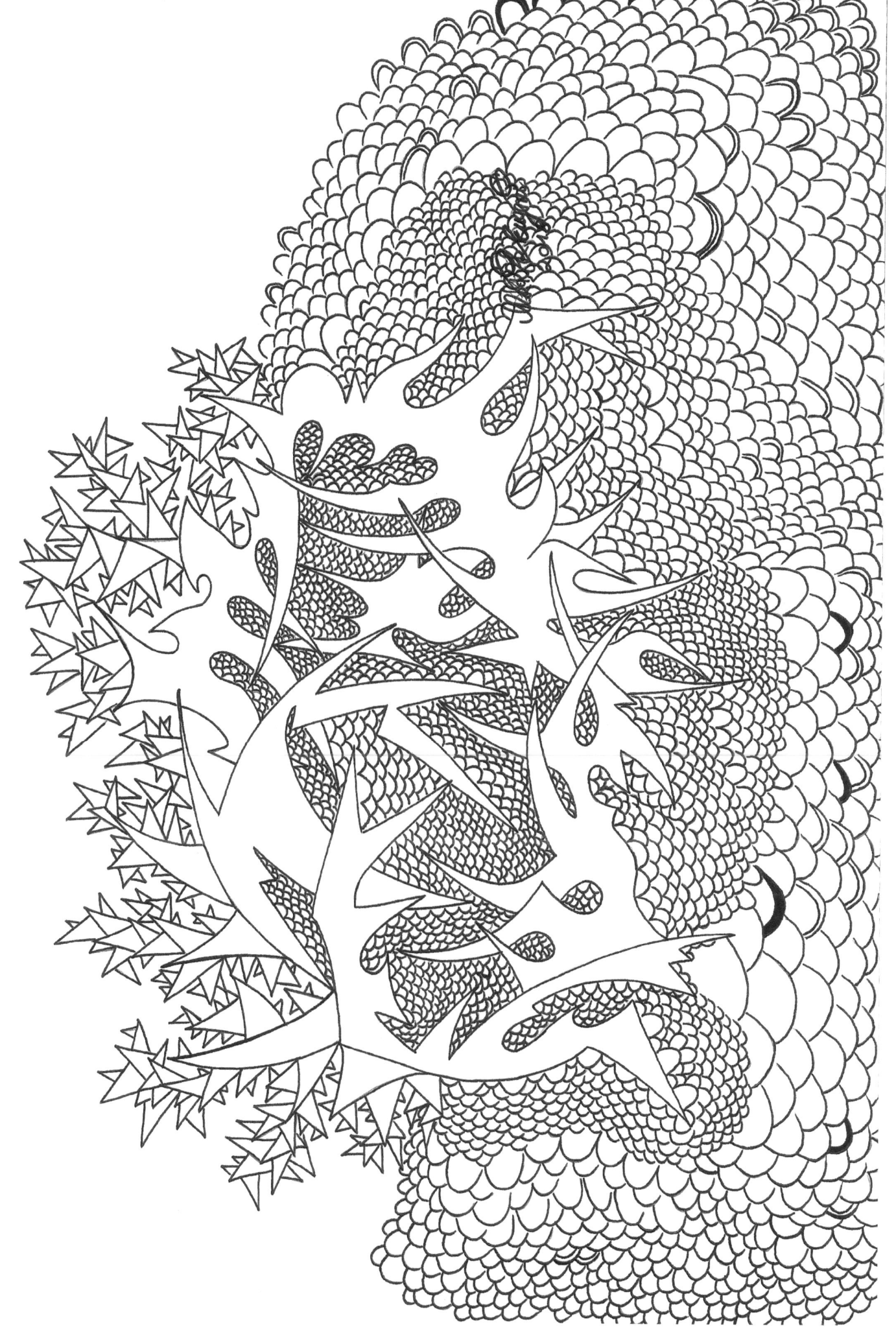

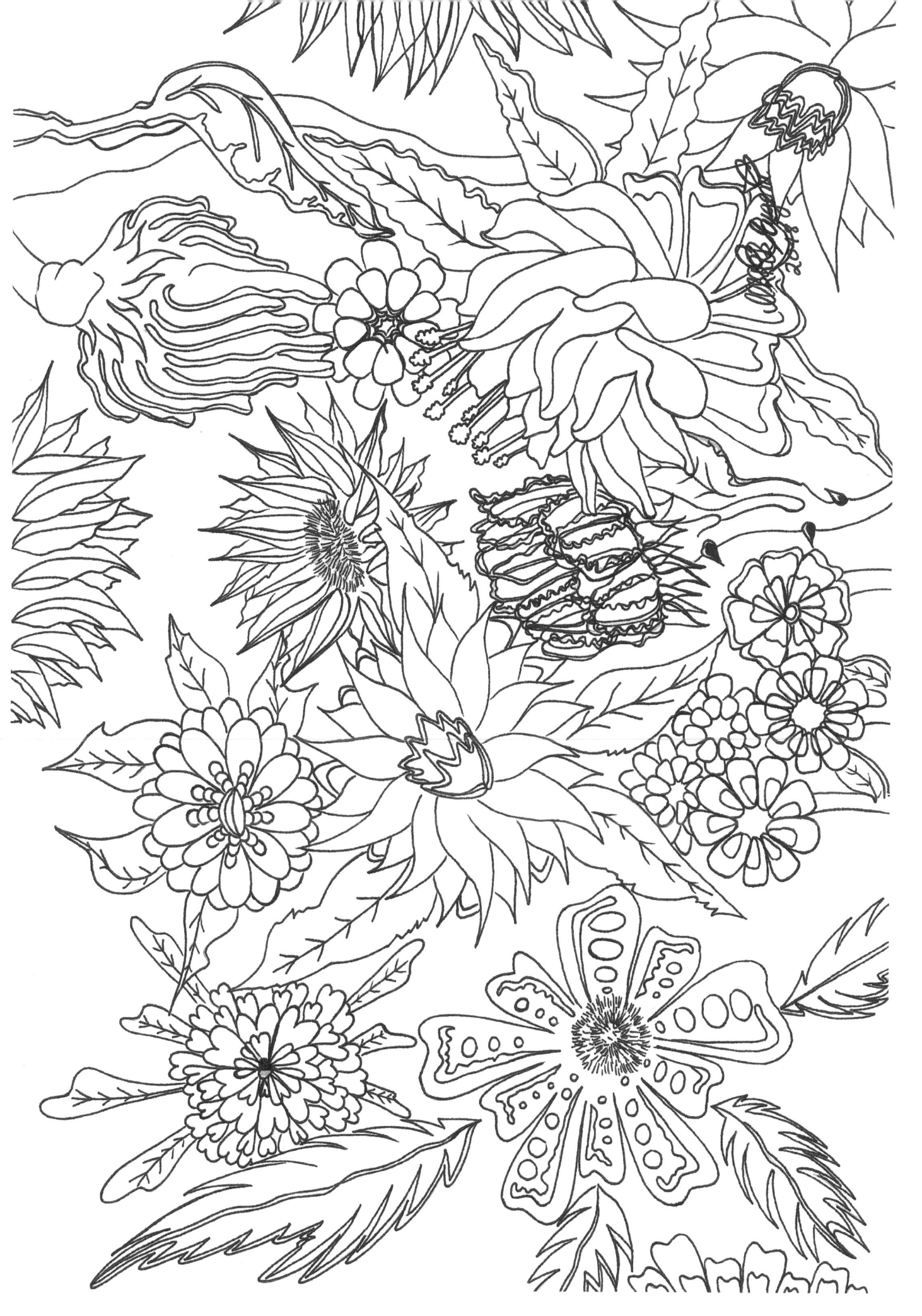

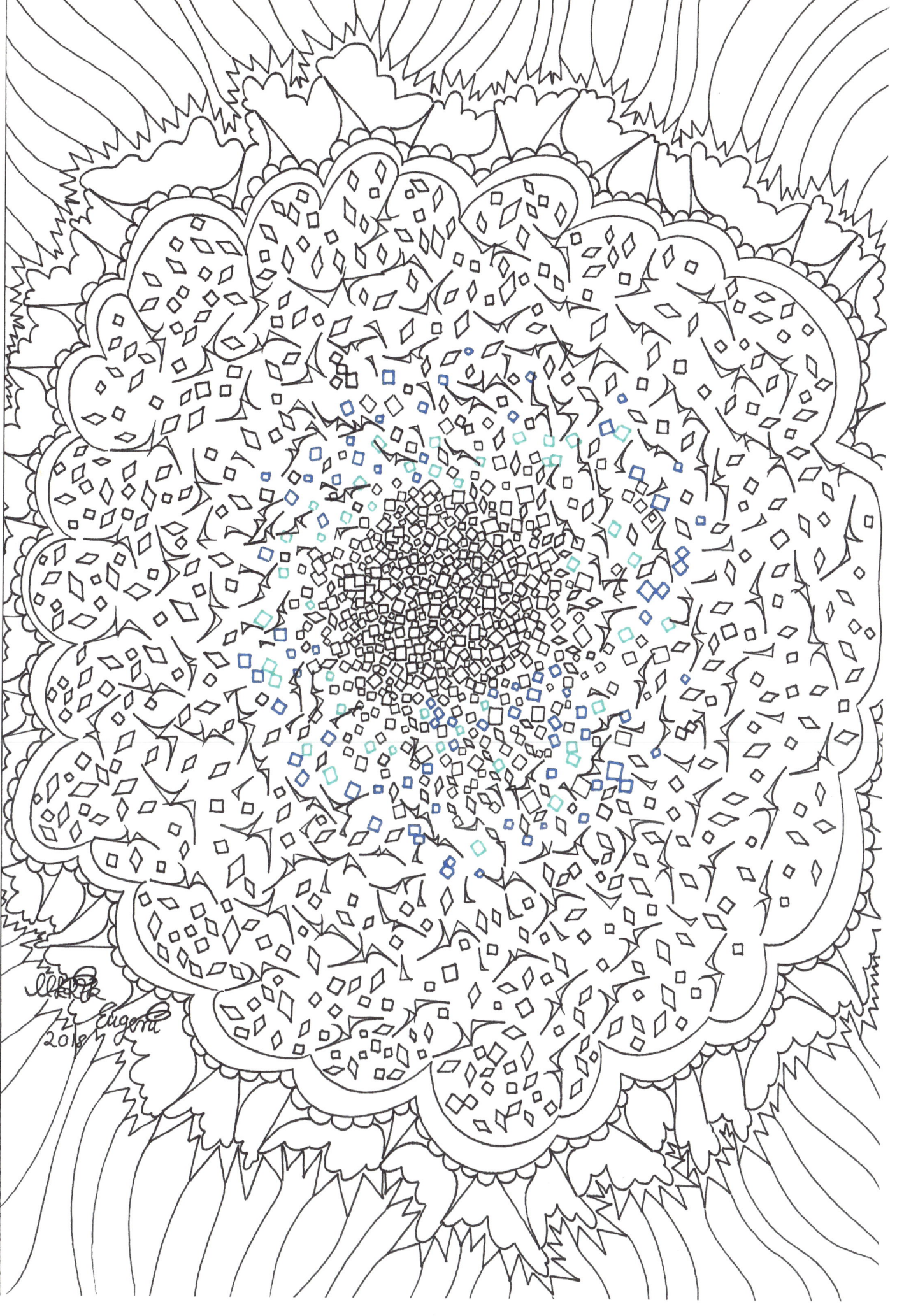

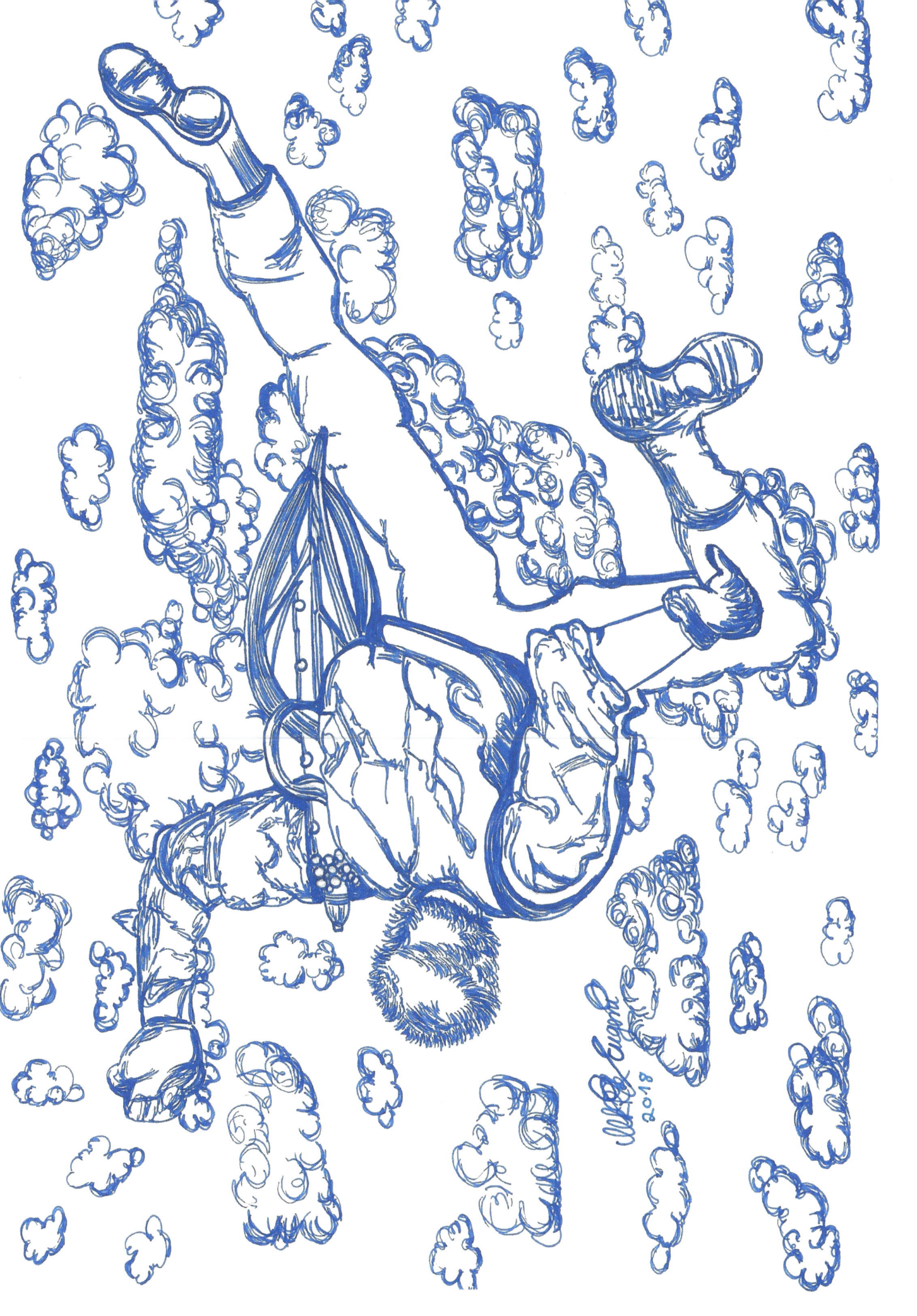

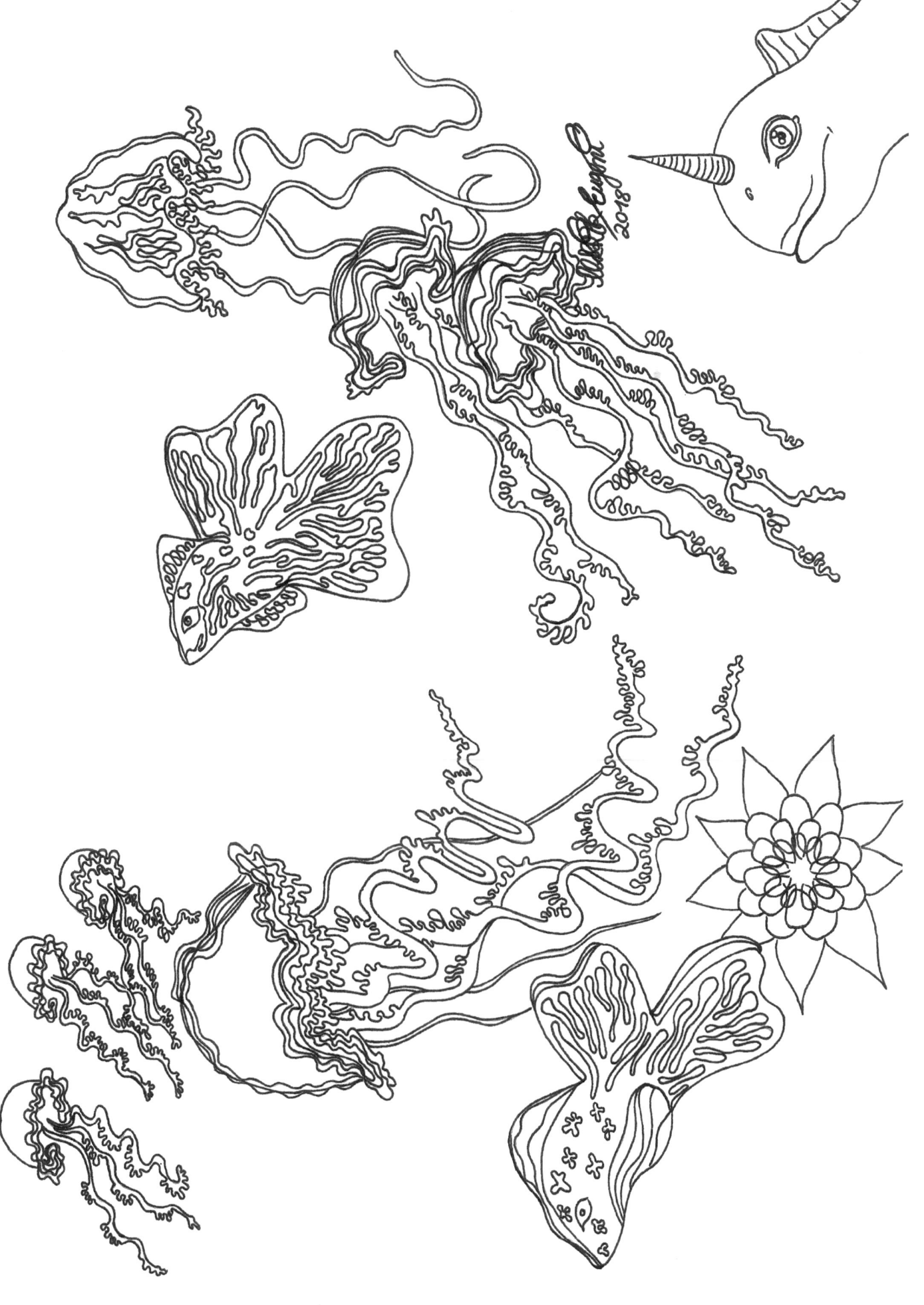

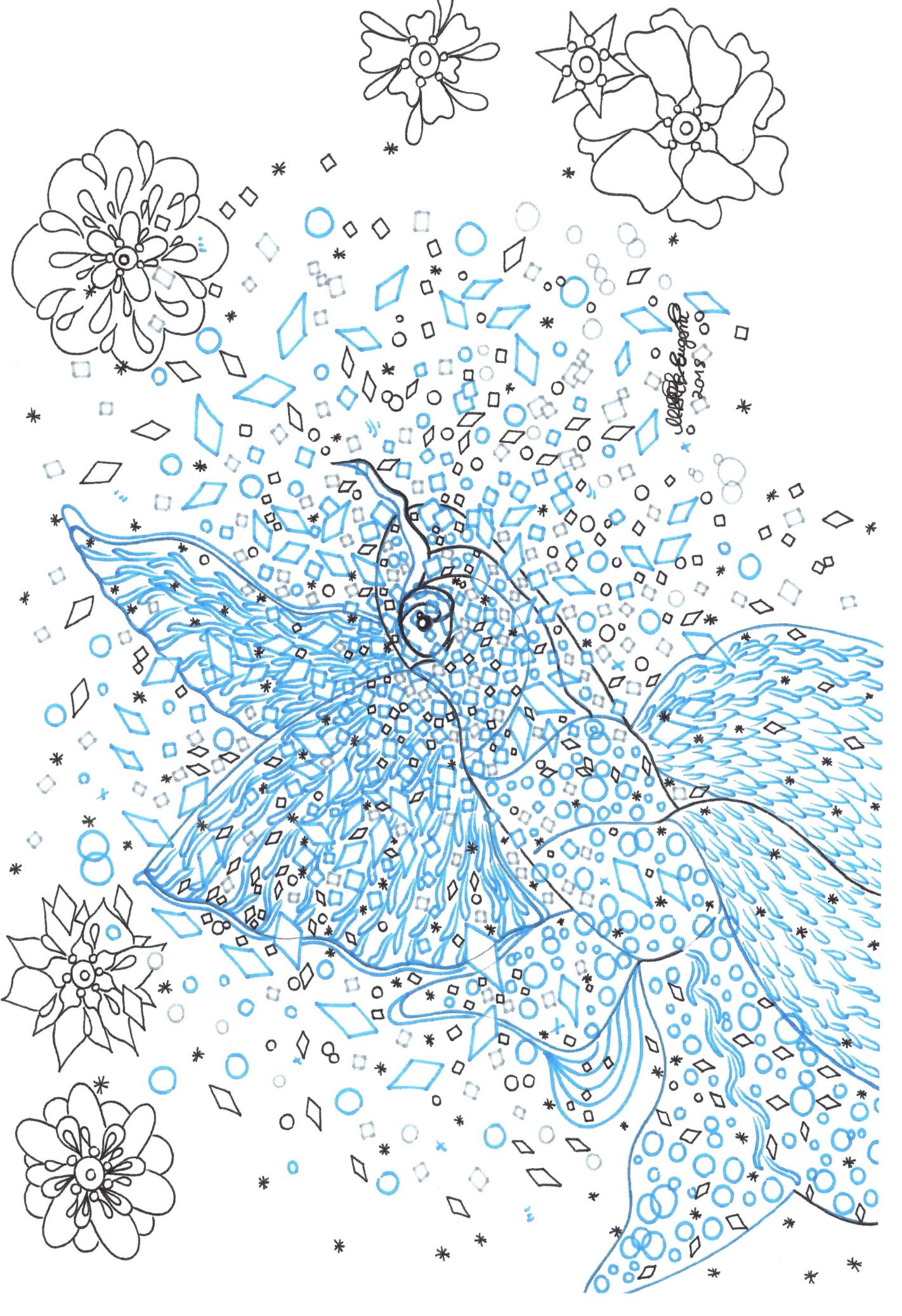

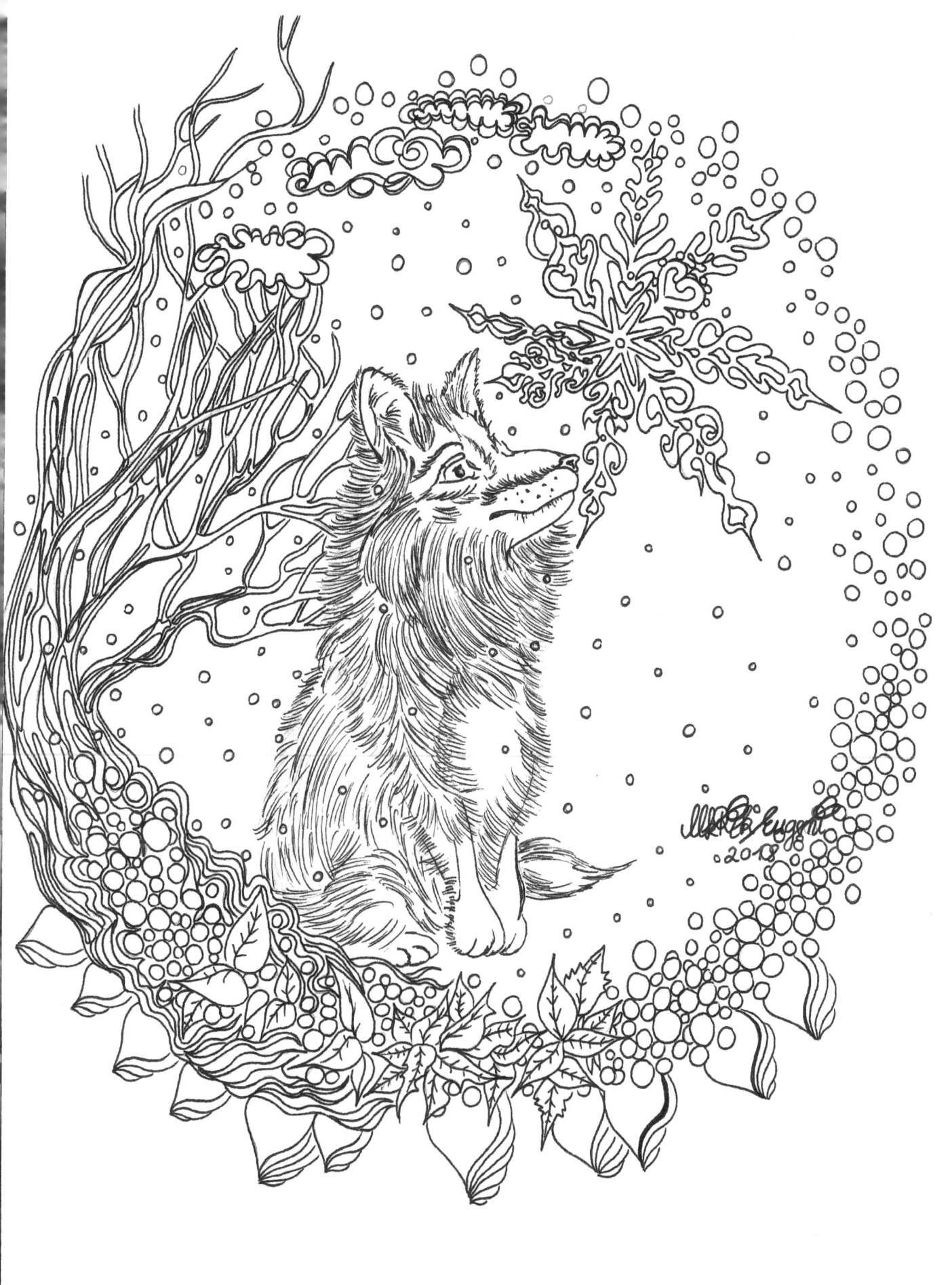

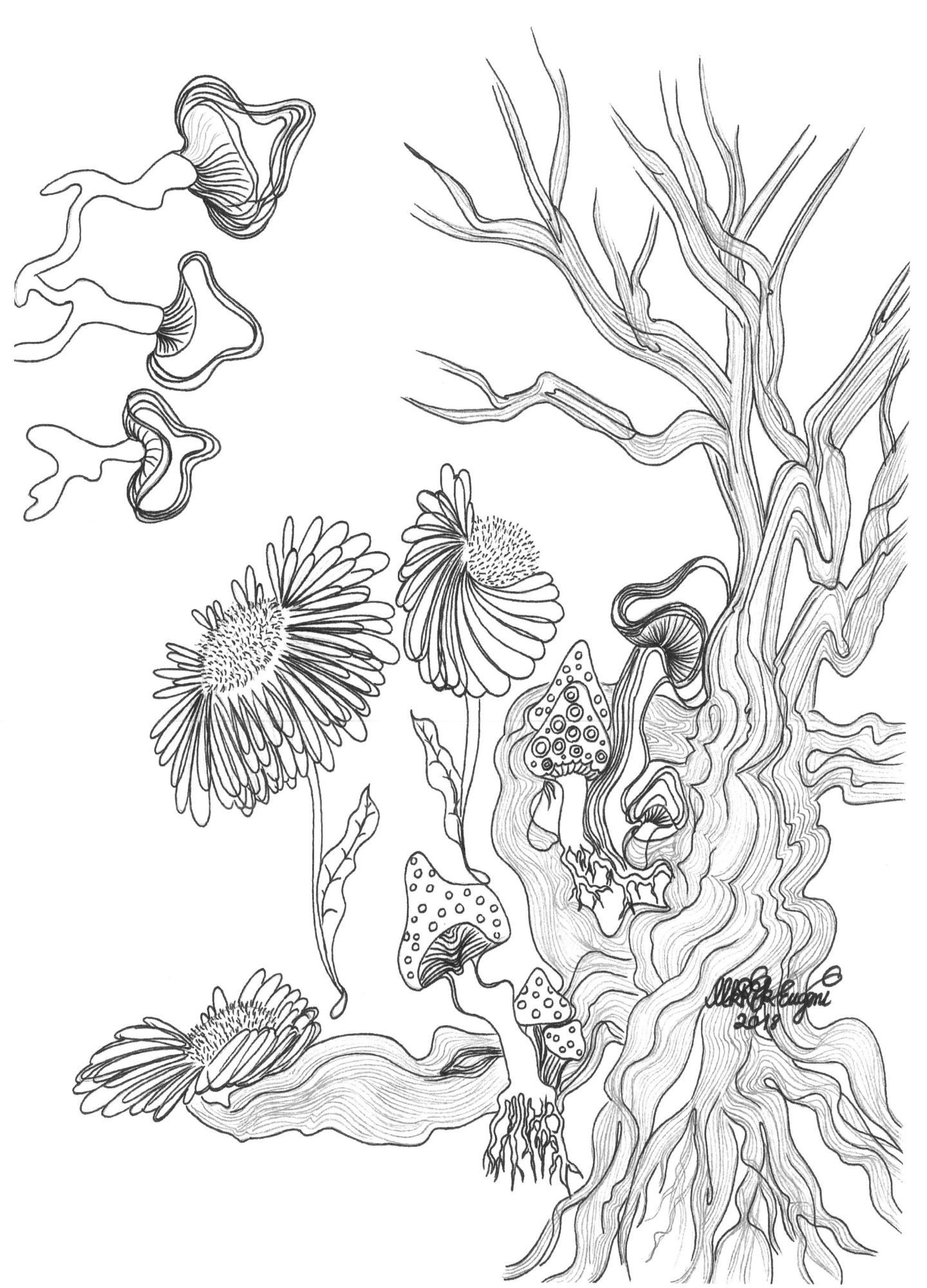

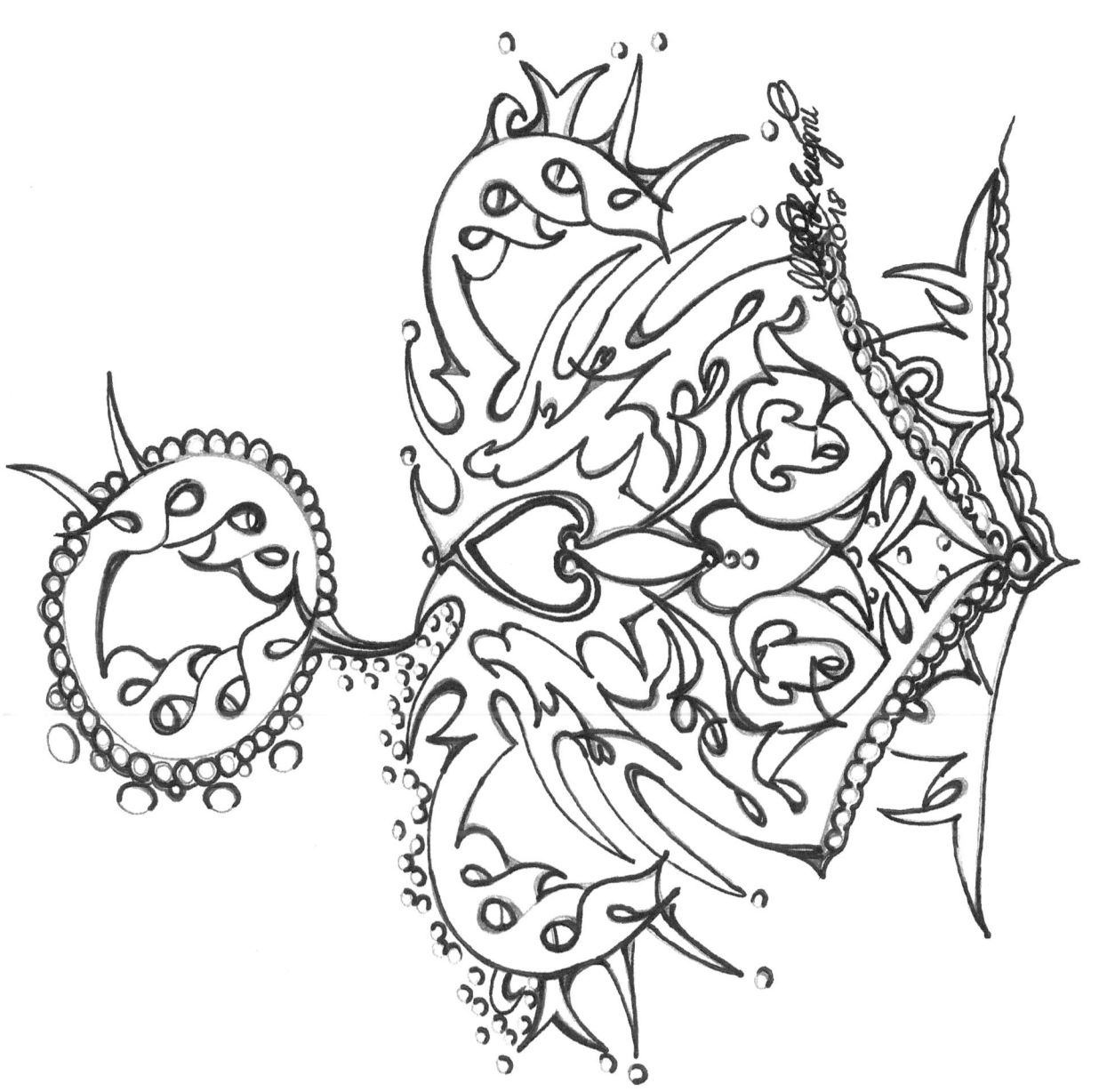

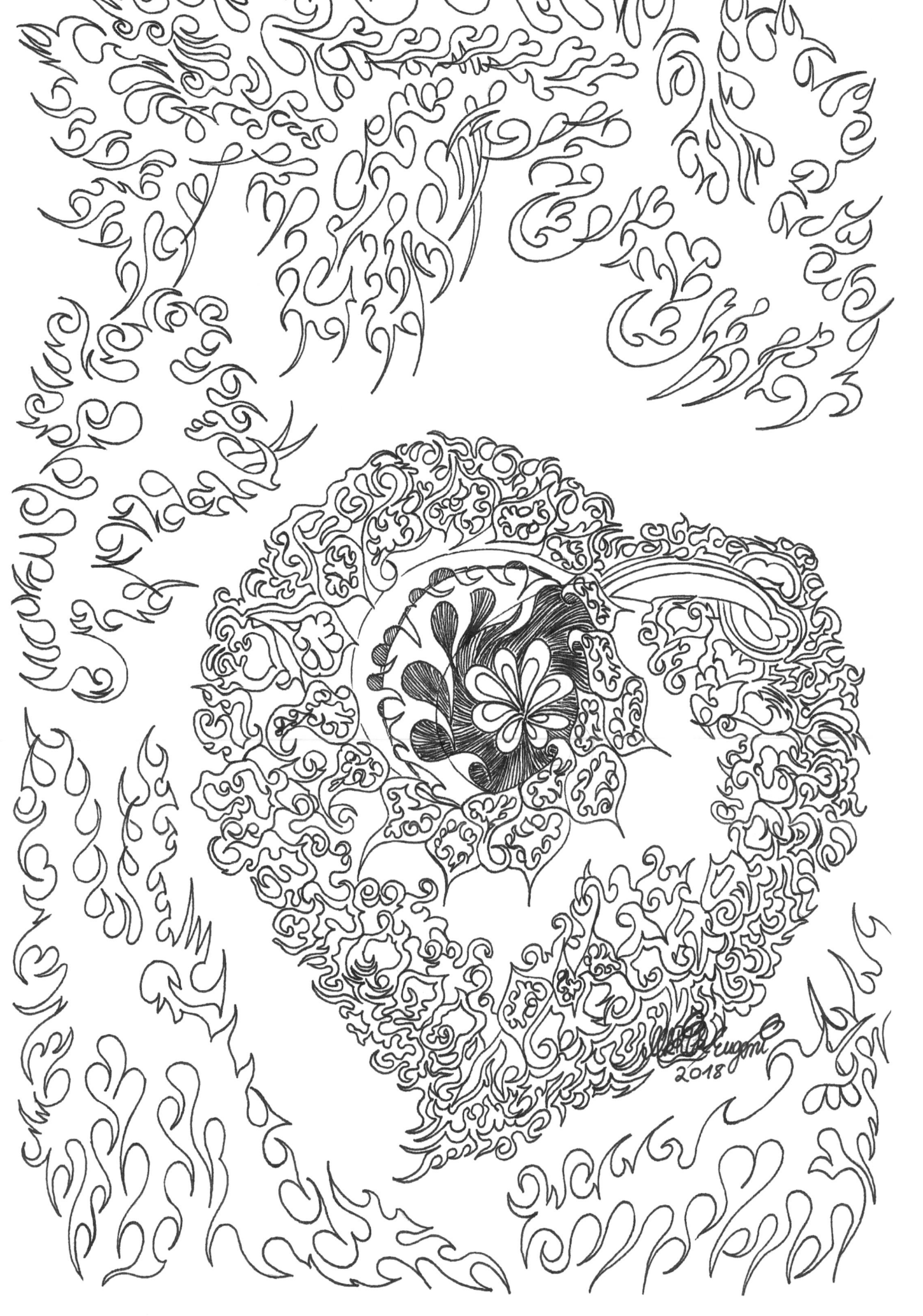

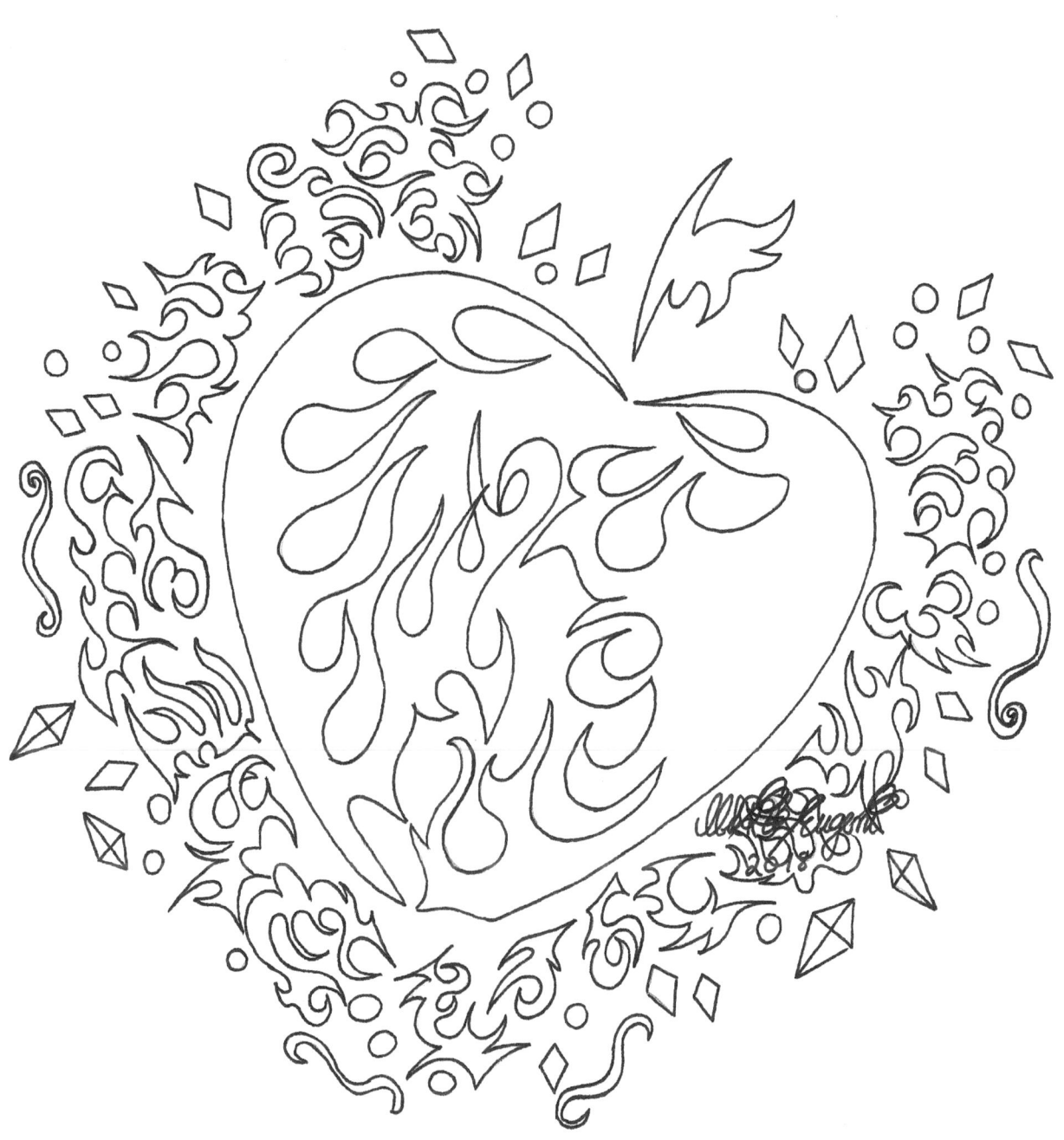

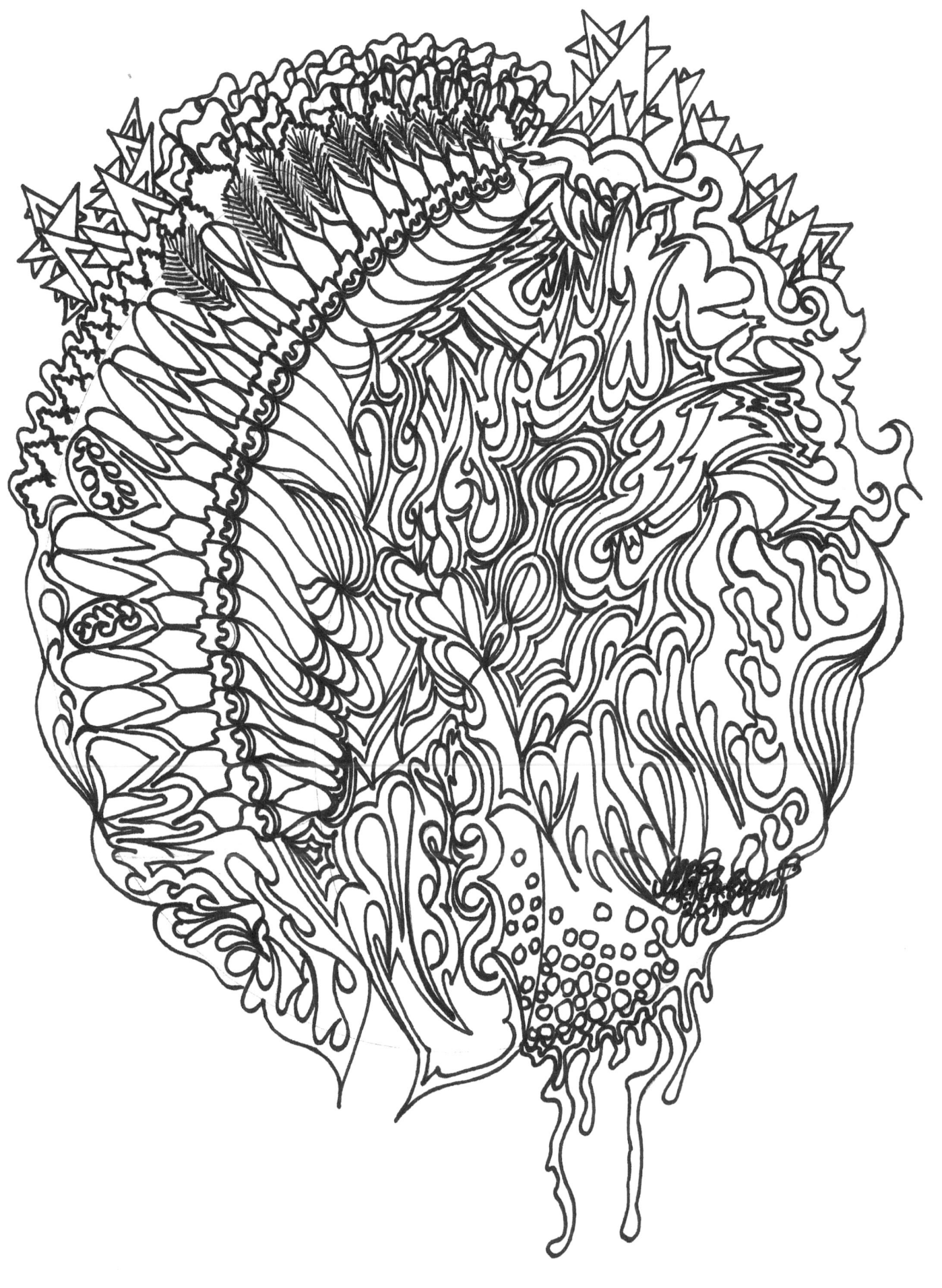

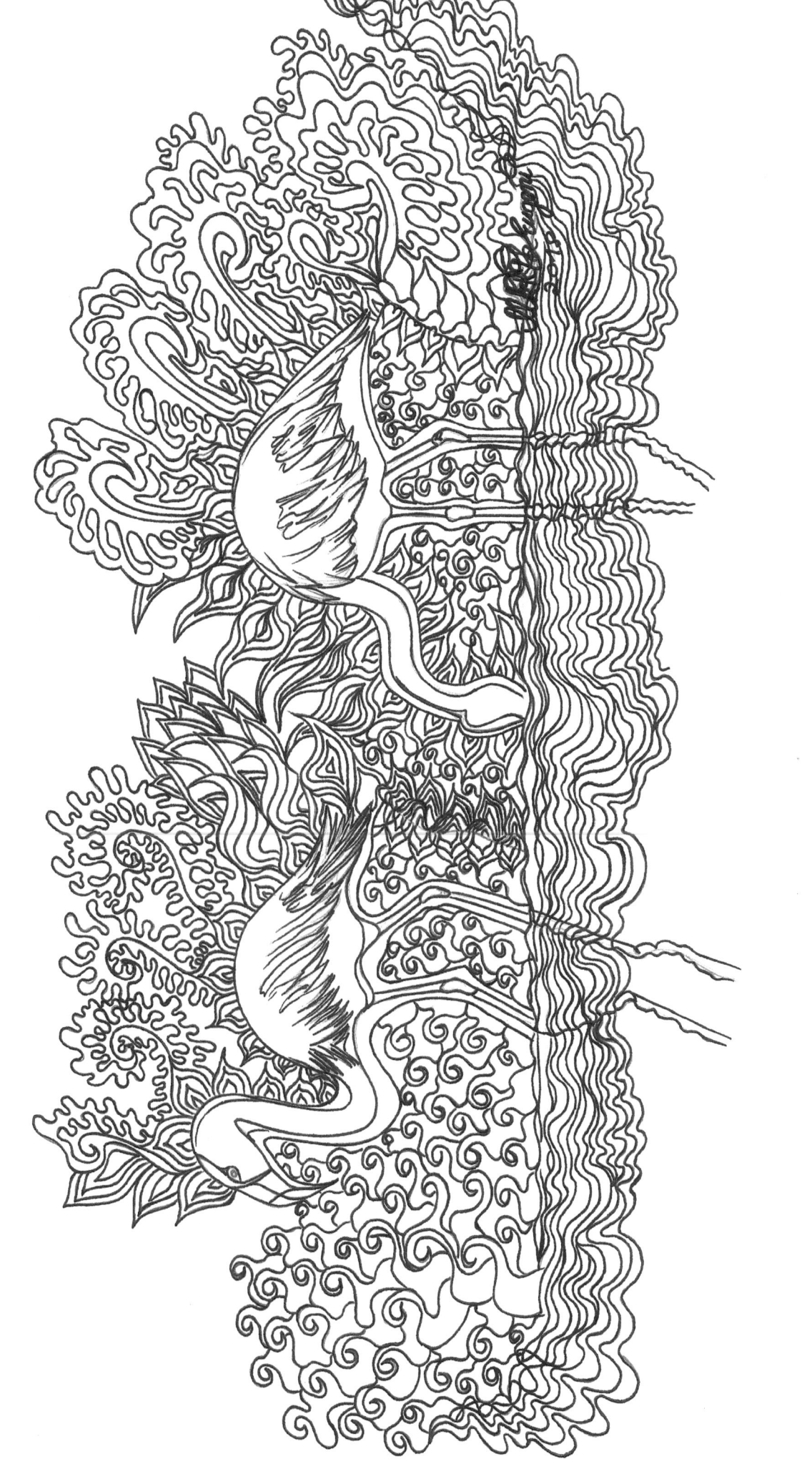

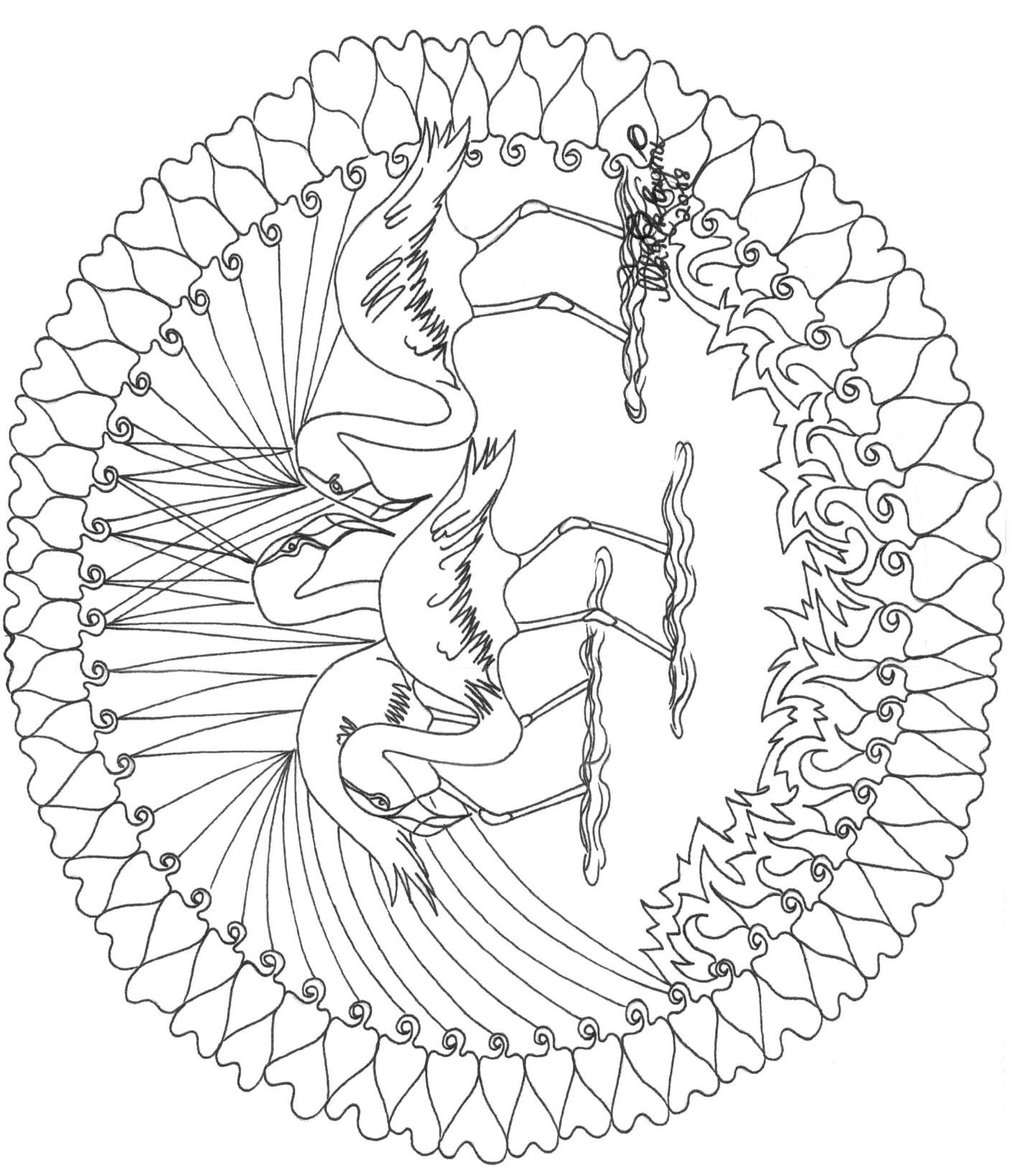

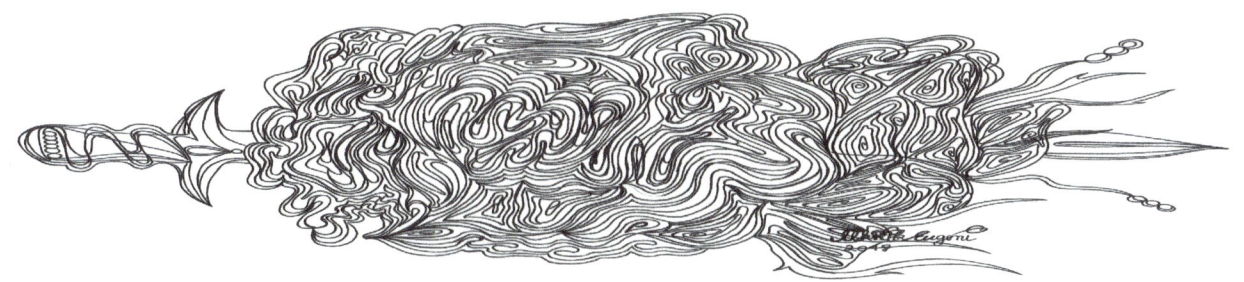

Thank You

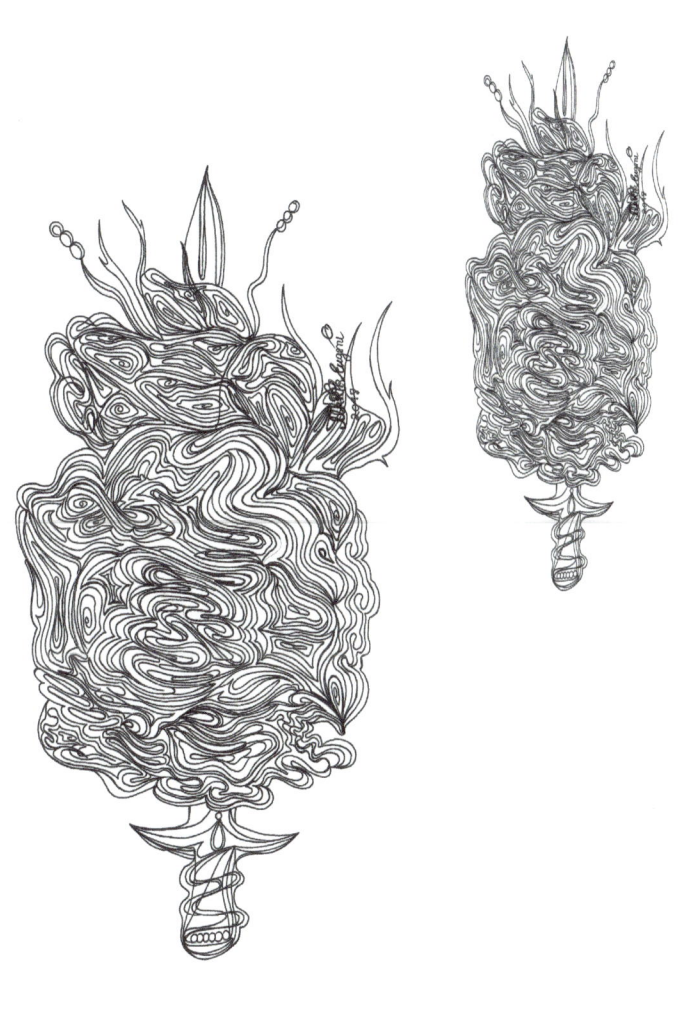
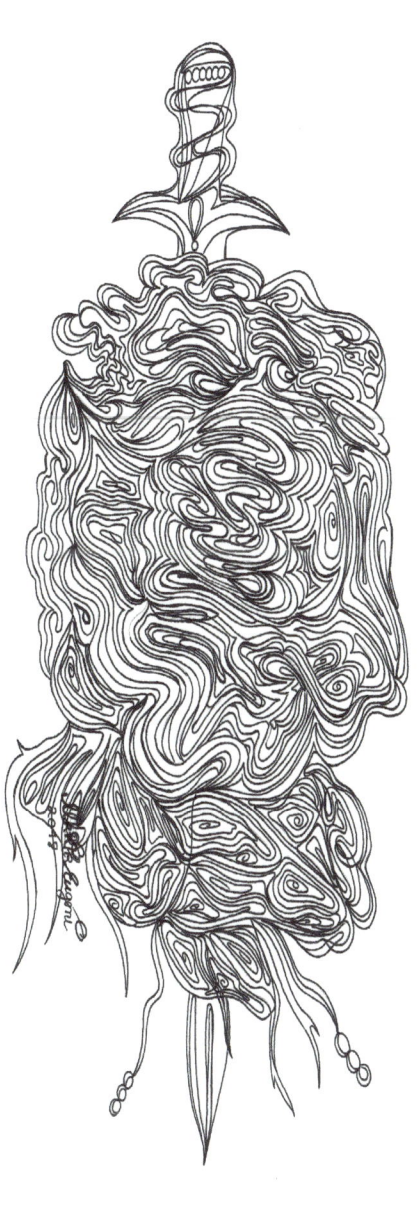

Adult Colouring Book

* Fine Art
* Fantasy
* Portrait
* Tattoo style
* Skull
* Animals
* Flowers
* Birds
* Figurative
* Shapes
* Cartoon
* Surrealism
* Abstract

Everyday is a new day, it can be Anything...........
Might you'll rich the Outer Limits with different Pictures !

Support & Like my Art Pages on :

Facebook : https://www.facebook.com/Marja777/

Follow me on Instagram : https://www.instagram.com/marjgeni/

www.ingramcontent.com/pod-product-compliance
Lightning Source LLC
Chambersburg PA
CBHW042321250526
R18347200001B/R183472PG45473CBX00004B/1